Handle Your Business

Handle Your Business

A Step-By-Step Blueprint for New Business Startups

Dr. Regina Banks-Hall

RBH Professional Publishing a division of RBH Professional Development Institute, LLC.

Southfield

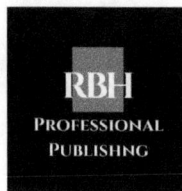

RBH Professional Development Institute, LLC., 2000 Town Center, 19th
Floor, Southfield, Michigan 48075

Dedication

Dedicated to all dreamers. Dedicated to those who desire more.

Contents

Acknowledgements

To my husband, thanks for your support and belief in my dreams. Thank you for reminding me, that I can achieve any goal I desire. I also want to thank you for reminding me that one of my gifts, is helping others succeed.

.

1

Introduction

Let me begin by asking you a question. When you think of a small business, how many of you think about a mom and pop store, restaurant, t-shirt shop, boutique, local diner, or bookstore? How many of you think to yourself, I could never start a business? Or, have you started a side business, and now you are ready to take that business to the next level, but the thought of moving forward is overwhelming? Whatever you are feeling, I want you to know that I have already been there, and I am here to help you.

Today, I would like to start out talking about small businesses. Small businesses are defined by many categories, and one of the messages that I always share with college students and coaching clients is that Amazon, Ford Motor Company, Apple, and Microsoft were all small businesses. The founders of these companies started with one concept and turned that concept into a global business success.

This book is designed to activate your best and most creative self. This book is for people who are ready to dust off their dreams and become business owners, authors, ministers, coaches, etc. This book is for people who are ready to change their lives. They are looking at the success of others and have determined it is time to launch their dreams.

As I think about my journey of launching a promotional products company, leadership development company, and publishing company, I remember the negative words shared with me. People, whether innocently, or on purpose, tried to convince me that success was not in my reach. They told me I was wasting my time. For a while, I listened to the voices of others who continued to crush my dreams. One day, I realized those individuals were trying to hold me back, and it was time to get busy with my life.

I began to list the things I wanted to do. I also remember having a lot of questions about business formation, taxes, etc. To my surprise, not many people wanted to share information. I joined associations, found mentors, and researched companies operating in my industry. I also learned through trial and error. Today, I still have questions, but through it all, I learned that it was important to remove negativity and follow my dreams.

Therefore, if you have been listening to negative people, tune them out. If you are stuck at a job you hate, stop wasting time, and energy complaining. Instead, think about something you are passionate about and focus on bringing that passion to life. The final point I want to make is, that it is okay to dream about wanting more.

As a business owner, college professor, author, certified trainer, and speaker, I encourage everyone who desires small business success, to start their journey and live out their dreams. Today, I have combined years of work experience and university teachings of Small Business Administration, Entrepreneurship, Human Resource Management, Marketing Management, Change Management, Leadership, Business Statistics, and Economics in preparing this book. In this book, I have focused on key areas every business owner must take note of while starting a new business.

Let's begin with some interesting facts about small

businesses. According to the Small Business Administration or SBA, Small Businesses:

- Employ 48% of all private-sector employees

- Pay 41.2% of total U.S. private payroll

- Created 63.3% of net new jobs over the past 20 years

- Created more than 50 percent of private gross domestic product (GDP)

Small businesses include home daycares, delivery services, t-shirt shops, transcription services, app providers, tutors, fast-food restaurants, carpenters, consultants, coaches, independent sales representatives, graphic artists, online gaming platforms, social media sites, professional service providers, and thousands of other titles.

Today, you may still be working a full-time job, ready to retire, about to graduate from college, or recovering from a job loss due to the pandemic. In the back of your mind, you have always had that business idea that keeps you up at night. This book was designed to help you find the courage to take that idea and turn it into reality. It will give you all of the key steps to launch your vision and start your journey.

It is my sincere hope that this book gives you the knowledge to make your decision, the passion to persevere, and the confidence to follow your dreams. Therefore, before you begin, take a moment to identify aspects of owning your own business, and how it will change your life.   What are the pros and cons of your decision? List them below.

Pros

_____

_____

_____

_____

_____

Cons

_____

_____

_____

_____

This exercise is important, because often when we look at the cons, the items we list are associated with a fear of success. The pros outweigh the cons when you think about how your business idea will change lives and bless others. Therefore, as we begin this journey, one of the first areas we have to change is our thinking.

The conversations we have with ourselves can have a dramatic impact on success. For myself, I learned to utilize the power of affirmations. Thus, now that you have identified the pros and cons, it is time to change your thinking. Therefore, I want to provide you with a list of affirmations that I want you to say to yourself.

- I believe in me

- I trust my abilities

- I will make a difference

- I am worthy of success

- I approve of myself

- I am walking in my purpose

- I provide value to my community

- I am making an impact in the lives of others

When you can change your thinking, you can begin to change how you will move forward with launching the business of your dreams. Positive affirmations allow you to begin the process of transformation. For anyone looking to change their destiny or change their current situation, it will require a change in your thinking. In the next chapter, we begin by talking about you.

2

Why Do You Want to Start A Business?

Are you like most people, who dream of seeing

their products on store shelves, the internet, or on the shop floor? Are you wondering how online sites, such as Chewy, Shopify, Amzaon, Etsy, and eBay created massive success? Are you passionate about an idea, but unsure of your next steps? If you have answered yes to these questions, I have some great news for you. You are like many people, who dream of entrepreneurship and desire a blueprint for moving forward. You spend the necessary time gathering information and now you are ready to start, yet something always seems to hold you back.

You have probably had this conversation with yourself, or someone else, about the risks of being an entrepreneur. You ask yourself, what if I fail? When you begin to think about it, working for someone else has some challenges also. The company can go out of business, decide to downsize or relocate. On the other hand, owning your own business can be an exhausting, yet rewarding experience. The question for you today is, what will you do?

Starting a business requires level headed thinking about the risks and rewards of entrepreneurship. It requires thoughtful planning and a dream. It is also important to emphasize that starting a business is not a get rich, quick scheme. For many people, entrepreneurship and small business ownership is the gateway to opportunity.

The key to successful entrepreneurship is, identifying a problem or concept others have overlooked and surround that idea with an effective strategy. After you have identified the problem, and have an effective strategy, you will be on your way to launching your idea.

Let's begin by defining an entrepreneur. An entrepreneur is a person who takes advantage of a business opportunity. This person assumes the financial and psychological risk of starting a company. Some characteristics of successful business owners include creativity, general management, performance, and innovation. Therefore, as you begin to think about your business idea or concept, begin to focus on some common sources for business idea formation.

Listed below are some common themes for creating your concept for a business:

- An emerging theme

- A gap in a specific industry

- A range of business offerings

- A product that helps others

- Special expertise you possess

- A problem that exists in your life.

- Prior work experience

Determine what your product or service is going to be, and most importantly, what it will not be.

Another area for idea creation is understanding the impact of your dreams. What are they? Are you visualizing yourself operating your new business? Are you dreaming about the impact this business will create for others? Ask yourself the following questions:

- What gives you a sense of satisfaction?

- What type of business could you immerse yourself in for forty, fifty, or sixty hours a week?

- What type of business would you be proud to share with others?

Now, take a moment to list your thoughts.

_____

_____

_____

_____

_____

After you have identified some potential ideas, it is now important for you to summarize your ideas and focus on creating an elevator pitch. This allows you to create a trial balloon for pitching your idea to potential customers or clients. The concept of what you want to do may still exist as a dream, but it is the crafted pitch or affirmation that will help keep a new business owner focused on the goal of starting the business. In short, the elevator pitch is simply a carefully crafted sentence that describes who you are and what you do.

For a new business owner, this elevator pitch is about your potential idea, and allows you a way to measure the feasibility of this idea becoming a real-world solution.

One good example is Warby Parker. This company was founded in 2010, by Neil Blumenthal, Andrew Hunt, David Gilboa, and Jeffrey Raider, and currently headquartered in New York City. The company's goal is to offer designer eyewear at "revolutionary prices leading the way for socially conscious businesses." In this example, Warby Parker has identified what the product is and what it is designed to do. Also, when you look at their business concept, they are solving two problems. The company significantly lowered the prices for glasses, and by donating a pair of glasses to those in need, they connect with socially driven consumers.

Take a moment and determine, what your product or service is, and what it will do. What makes it unique? What makes it relevant? List your answers here:

_____

_____

_____

_____

_____

In the introduction, I talked about my personal journey. As I look back, I have identified crucial steps that many entrepreneurs use to achieve their goals. The first step is that you must believe you can. Your belief in your abilities is important. It is this belief that keeps you moving forward when you are ready to give up. The second step is, you must create a plan. We have seen it a thousand times, planning + action = success.

The third step is important and often overlooked. The third step is seeking out help. As new business owners, we must add mentors and other successful like-minded people to our inner circle. This can be accomplished by joining associations, chambers of commerce, and attending networking events, where you network with other business owners.

The fourth step requires that you create a mentality to do well. As a new business owner, think about your stakeholders, suppliers, customers, and employees, who are depending on the success of your business. When you take the focus off yourself and place the focus on others, that will give you the energy you need to succeed.

The fifth and final step in this process requires that the new business owner engages in a check and balance system for success. The process includes the following steps: belief, test, prepare, and execute. The belief principle recognizes your willingness to start a business. You have an idea, and you are ready to act upon it. The test principle requires that you engage in a feasibility analysis to see what you know related to your business idea. When you apply the preparation principle you are crafting ways to provide your product. Your plan may include a product offering or test market to see how your product comes to life. Finally, in the execution phase, you continue to review and refine your idea until you create a winning formula.

This brings me to another business success story I would like to share with you. Our subject here is Aaron Patzer, the founder of the web-based personal finance service Mint.com. Aaron shared that he started the company because he could not manage his finances using Quicken and Microsoft Money. At the time, they had no mobile app. Aaron created this business to solve a convenience problem of his own. The incredible part of this story is that Aaron would go on to sell Mint to Intuit for $170 million.

Therefore, as you begin to think about your new business idea, view your new venture through the lens of creating a new market, new technology, or new benefit. Each business idea provides its unique features during the discovery phase. Let's begin with a discussion on new market ideas.

The first new market idea is to provide customers with a product or service that does not exist in a particular market but can exist somewhere else. Here the business owner can take an idea that exists and apply that idea within a new context. For example, when I started RBH Professional Development, leadership and training were offered on many platforms, but none I researched offered publishing services. Seeing this deficiency, I made this my niche. I took an existing concept and expanded it.

The second business idea involves new technology. Technology ideas focus on providing customers or businesses with a new product or service. One of the most successful technological ideas was the creation of Stash. Stash was created by Brandon Kreigh, Ed Robinson, and David Ronick. Stash allows consumers to purchase fractional shares of stock as a way to build their wealth. Again, purchasing stock was available on many platforms, but not by fractional shares. Another example of a technology business idea that I would like to mention is Ring.com. The Company Ring was founded in 2012 by Jamie Siminoff. Through crowdfunding, the company raised over $300,000. In 2013, the company released a doorbell with internet connectivity, high definition camera, and a motion detector. These components existed on many platforms but not with this concept. Ring was purchased by Amazon in 2018 for the estimated value of $1.2 Billion.

The third idea centers on benefits. Benefit ideas provide customer benefits from new or improved products and services. Benefit ideas also provide a better way of performing current functions. The best example that comes to mind is Amazon, launched by Jeff Bezos in 1994 as an online marketplace for books. They eventually went on to expand their business, providing things like electronics, food, music, apparel, and toys. Their two-day delivery option is considered an improved service benefit. Currently, they are considered by business experts as one of the largest online marketplaces in the world with a revenue of $280 Billion (2019 estimates) and provides over 12 million products.

As you look at each type of business idea, it is important to note that your idea can come from your past work experience, hobby, suggestion, inconvenience, education, friend, or my favorite, by accident. If you are struggling to create your idea, commit to thinking creatively as you look at the world around you. First focus on finding your niche. Some of the best ideas can come from your strongest areas of interest. Take a moment to answer the following questions:

What are your hobbies?

_____

_____

_____

_____

_____

How do you love to spend your time?

_____

_____

_____

_____

_____

What is your current work experience?

_____

_____

_____

_____

_____

Name some things that irritate you?

_____

_____

_____

_____

_____

What great ideas can come from what you have listed above?

_____

_____

_____

_____

_____

You can also think about combining two business ideas into one. When you combine two business ideas, you can create a unique product, service, or experience. Some examples include Barnes and Noble's addition of a coffee shop within the bookstore, or a theater venue that adds a nice sit-down dinner before the show.

Another great idea is to begin with the problem in mind. Think about a problem you have, or a problem that you believe affects others. How would you solve this problem, and why does this problem need solving? As you begin to focus on solving this particular problem, many ideas can be generated.

As you are thinking about your new idea, it will be important for you to separate trends from fads. Trends are connected to a larger change in society's thinking. Fads are short-lived money-making opportunities, that will quickly fade when the luster of the fad diminishes. For example, the success of Facebook,

Twitter, and YouTube represents a change in society's thinking, whereas, clothing trends would represent fads. If you choose to create your business from a fad, be prepared to pivot quickly to the next big thing.

My final recommendation is to explore ways to improve an existing product or service. One example, I would like to discuss is leasing office space. For individuals who provide office space as a business, their products and service were often viewed through one lens. Business owners either started with a home office or leased office space. As a tenant, you were saddled with a high monthly rental expense.

Now small business owners can rent an office, co-working space, business lounge, rent by the hour, or on a month to month contract. This change in coworking spaces has allowed small business owners to have a professional address for their business, and a place to meet with clients while reducing cost. This change in service has created a win/win for both the rental company and the tenant. Providing these rental options, as a business owner, can be a very lucrative idea.

The next area you must focus on is creating an internal and external assessment for your idea. The business owner must assess the general business environment and determine how the current business environment impacts the business idea. The business owner must also evaluate any technological requirements for launching a new business idea. Finally, the business owner must evaluate how the economy will affect the business, identify the competitive landscape, and determine if there are any political or legal issues associated with the success of the new business idea.

As a business professor, one of the things I love to share with students, or in my small business workshops, are the five competitive forces introduced by Michael Porter in his 1988 book, *Competitive Strategy: Techniques for Analyzing Industries and Competitors.* In his book, Michael talks about the business landscape and advises business owners and organization leaders to assess their strengths and weaknesses. Listed below are areas from the book that are important for all new business owners to consider.

1. The threat of new entrants: How easily can someone enter your marketplace?

2. How can customers bypass you with other options?

3. What is the impact of your customers' bargaining power?

4. What is the bargaining power of your suppliers?

5. How many competitors operate in your marketplace?

Micheal was recommending that new businesses understand how these critical areas can impact the success of their product or service. By understanding these five competitive forces, you can lay the foundation for launching a successful business.

This chapter focused on the concept of crafting your business idea. As you move forward reading this book, we will focus in greater detail on aspects concerning, customers, credit, competence, competition, business formation, and financial statements.

3

Defining Your Customer

After you have defined your business idea it is now time to identify the market which contains your customers. When you think about the market for your product or service, you need to focus on two main areas. These two areas are mass-markets or niche markets. Mass markets involve large portions of a population. A niche market is a defined segment of the population that is likely to share the same interests or concerns.

If your business idea focuses on a niche market, you will focus on the customers in that niche market.

Once you have determined the type of market, you must now determine what your product or service will provide. Therefore, it is important to identify the type of customer you are looking for. Are you looking for a corporate customer? Are you looking for online customers? Are you looking for local customers? Are you looking for loyal customers? After you determine your customer's type, you can begin working on your strategy to find those customers. This will also help you tailor your product or service to your customer.

Another critical component, when focusing on your customers, is identifying the value proposition of the product or service that you provide. The value proposition are the features that make your product or service attractive to your customer. In other words, what's the benefit? Benefits are the characteristics that define your product or service. The benefit is often defined as a value or cost-benefit. A value benefit relates to the nature of the product or service. Some value benefits are fashion, reputation, and quality. Understanding the value of a product or service as a business owner is a critical component of success. This understanding can lead to higher prices and higher profits.

Cost benefits define ways the firm keeps the cost low for the customer. Some cost benefits allow customers to buy in volume, which produces savings. For example, Costco and Sam's Club provide a variety of services. Customers can purchase food for the home, hearing aids, tires, and eyeglasses from the same location. They also provide businesses the opportunity to purchase business-to-business services for their organizations. Therefore, as you look at your business idea, determine if you can connect multiple product offerings that create cost benefits.

The next area of focus is on understanding product reviews. Reviews on sites like Amazon and eBay allow customers to rate a product or service. Customers will visit sites such as Yelp or Angie's List and leave an opinion for a product or service they have received. This is important for restaurants, hotels, and cellular phone providers such as Verizon and T-Mobile. The ratings and complaints about products can give you information on what people like or dislike. As a new or expanding business, understanding reviews can provide helpful information as you continue to craft or improve your product idea.

Let's now discuss an important benefit. That benefit is quality. When you think about your product, what quality separates your product from your competitor? Will you associate the quality of your product with the price? Some quality examples include Coach handbags, Apple Products, and Nike Products. These name brands are associated with dependability, durability, and elite customer service. These qualities help to establish their upscale pricing.

Another valued benefit is service. Are you providing personalized service, where you remember the customer's name? Are you providing door-to-door services, such as Doordash or Uber Eats? Are you promoting a concept of providing service in a few minutes, or will you offer unconditional guarantees if the customer is not satisfied? Another valued benefit focuses on technology. Will you offer state of the art or leading-edge technology? Will your technology automate the process, or provide complementary services such as an automated attendant?

Another benefit that separates businesses is the delivery of the product. This can be challenging depending on the type of product or service. Therefore, determine if you will offer expedited services. For example, will you follow Amazon's business model of two-day delivery, or do you believe that offering delivery of the product is the benefit itself?

Another valued benefit that is important to evaluate is altruism. Altruism takes place when the product or service helps the community, the environment, or the world. Determine if part of what you provide fits this category. This can be important for customers who want organizations to focus on social issues. One good example of an organization that operates effectively in this area is Ben & Jerry's Ice Cream. Often when people think of Ben & Jerry's they only think about ice cream. However, Ben & Jerry's organization has a strong commitment to the environment, and it is evident on their website.

The final area of value that I want to focus on is brand and reputation. For a new business, referrals and testimonies from existing customers will help you build your brand. For an established company, the focus is on creating strategies that maintain the brand. Therefore, focus on a compelling strategy that supports brand/reputation. By conducting some research on your potential product or service, you can determine your strategy for entering the market and targeting the right customer. This will allow you to receive the benefits from the product or service you offer.

In the final section of this chapter, I want to focus on market research as it relates to finding customers. Market research allows you to identify your target audience. When you can identify your target audience you can now create key messages, features, and benefits that will matter to them. The question that you must ask yourself is, how can you compete in fulfilling their current needs, yet offer options and innovations that they are not currently receiving from the competition? For example, if you are starting a new T-shirt company, what different processes, innovations, and t-shirt ideas separate you from what currently exists in that local marketplace.

The next question is how do they currently obtain this product or service? If you provide the product or service, how will you deliver it differently or more affordably? How can you make it easier to obtain, or deliver it faster? In defining the customer, the business owner should be as accurate as possible, as that will support your market research and build on repeat customers. Listed below are some common practices that support finding customers for your product.

1.   **Referrals and reviews:** Using business contacts who are happy with your service will help generate referrals. Happy customers can help you sell your products or services by providing testimonials You can also use a refer-a-friend campaign by providing discounts. This is also an effective word of mouth advertising method.

2.   **Networking** – Create a goal to meet new contacts on a daily, weekly, and monthly basis. Attend Chamber of Commerce Meetings and join Professional Associations. Utilize social media sites to promote your product and make connections.

3.   **Affinity groups.** Affinity groups are formed around a shared interest or common goals. One group I want to mention is the National Association of Women Business Owners. Their activities all support the development of female-owned businesses. In this case, if you are a female business owner, this would be a great place to promote your product or service and find new customers.

4.   **Cold Calling** – Cold Calling is one of the oldest methods in the book. You pick up the phone, and contact individuals promoting your service. I can remember in the early days of my business, contacting strangers was the toughest business function I had to master. However, I would eventually overcome this issue. When using this method, please research the organization before you make your first call. It is also important to create a script that you can use continuously. I recommend you create a script that is simple

and outlines your objectives. Last of all, be friendly. You win more bees with honey.

5. **Direct Email** – As we move into the 21st century another helpful customer sourcing method is to cold call by direct email. When using this approach, you can promote a complimentary offer, discount, link to your website, or a new training program. This method can also be used continuously to introduce new products and share additional information regarding your business.

6. **Advertising** – For a new business owner, advertising has to be effective and cost-efficient. As a business owner, it will be important to determine how much of your revenue should be allocated for advertising. As the business grows, you will be able to increase your advertising budget. Therefore, please think about your customer when determining your advertising method. For example, if you are targeting Generation X or Millennials, online advertising using Google's AdWords, continues to be a favorite by many businesses.

Another form of online advertising is Social Media Promotions on Facebook, WordPress, Tumblr, Instagram, Pinterest, and Twitter. These platforms can increase your exposure. One of my favorite methods is the use of an online email distribution list. An online email distribution list, allows you to collect information about potential customers that can be used for advertising and promotion of your products. This list allows you to communicate with your customers and find leads regularly. Some email distribution platforms are Mailchimp and Constant Contact.

7.   **Market Research** – A final area of developing customers requires you to develop a solid marketing research campaign.   Understanding Market research allows you to learn more about your customer.   One of the easiest ways to conduct market research is by providing your customers with a survey.   Their responses will allow you to evaluate your marketing campaign. You can use online tools such as SurveyMonkey. You can also use government resources such as the U.S. Census Bureau, trade associations, or information from research firms, which can provide you with information concerning demographics, culture, attitudes, and buying habits.   The type of information you will receive will focus on the research questions you are asking and the resources allocated for those services.

When you understand your key target market, you can determine how to craft your messages, features, and promote the benefits of your product.   You can let your customers know how your product solves their problem.   Thus, reinforcing the value proposition your product or service provides.

4

Competition

Now that you have decided to start a business, it is time to identify the competition. When looking at your competitors, small business owners have to be strategic in their approach.

Small business owners must know how to navigate when you are entering a crowded market.

A competitive advantage is that unique edge that allows your business to attract more customers, or achieve greater sales over your competitors. This competitive advantage can mean the difference between your company being considered an average business, or your company leading the pack.

As you think about your competitive advantage, you want to have a strategy for the following:

- **Price**

- **Distribution Channel**

- **Customer Service**

- **Personal skill, knowledge, and ability**

- **Strategic partnerships**

- **Market Awareness**

Another key variable is understanding the competitive nature of a market's industry, as you must be aware of the forces that work against you. Earlier I mentioned Michael Porter and his five competitive forces. The key driving force behind the Five forces is to determine the attractiveness of a market's industry. The industry is attractive if the five forces are arranged in a manner that supports profitability. The industry is unattractive if the forces are connected in a manner that causes profitability to drop.

Now let's take a deeper dive as I explain the impact of these forces as they fight to undermine your competitive edge.

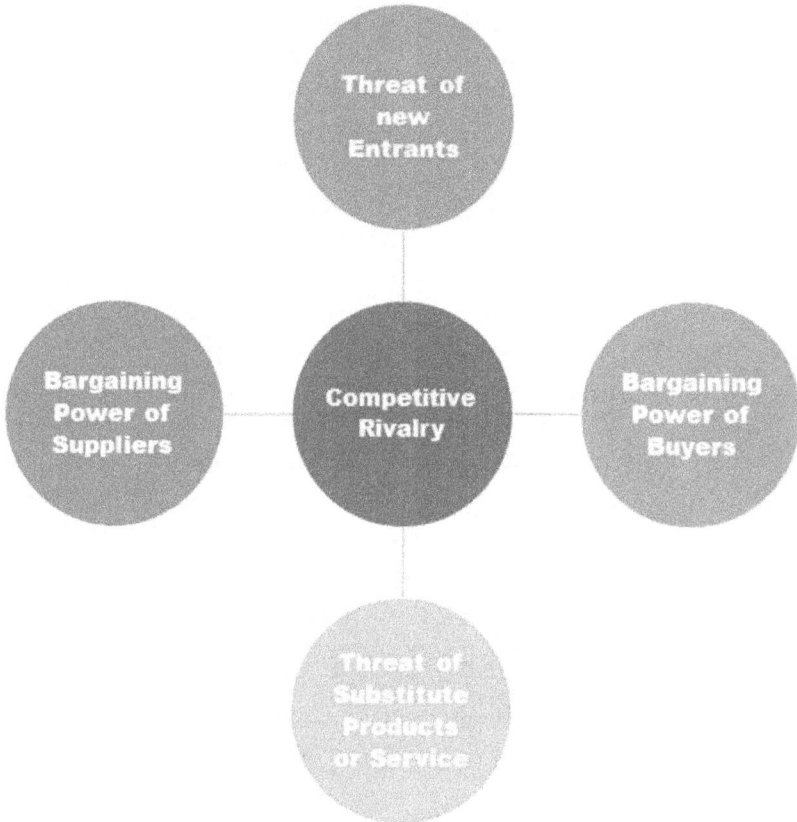

Adaptation of the Five Competitive Forces

1. **New Entrants to the market** – The threat of new entrants exist in all markets. New entrants in an industry bring new capacity and a desire to gain market share. That desire puts pressure on prices, costs, and the rate of investment necessary to

compete. Industry attractiveness increases when there are barriers to entry. How easily can a new competitor enter your market? Do others operating in the market face significant barriers?

2. **Substitute products** – A substitute product performs the same or a similar function as an industry's leading product, through different means. In an industry with a high threat of substitute products, the original product can lose its value. You will want a strategy that protects you from substitutes eating away at your business.

3. **Customer power** – Buyers are powerful if they have negotiating leverage relative to industry participants. This leverage can impact your ability to set and maintain prices for your products. How much control do you, as the owner, have over setting the prices for your products? Can your customers force you to offer your product at less than its value?

4. **Power of Suppliers** – Powerful suppliers capture more value for themselves by charging higher prices, thus, limiting quality or services. Also, powerful suppliers often shift costs to industry participants. How much power do suppliers have at setting prices and market conditions for your business?

5. **Competitive Rivalry** – Rivalry among existing competitors can take on many different forms,

including price discounting, new product introductions, advertising, and service improvements. High rivalry can limit the profitability of an industry. The strength of rivalry reflects the intensity and basis of competition. The dimensions on which competition takes place, and how rivals converge to compete, can have a major influence on profitability. Therefore, you must determine how many powerful competitors operate in your market? Will your relationship with them be civil or vicious?

Let's take a look at the following business case example.

BUSINESS CASE EXAMPLE

If you are opening up a t-shirt shop, you want to know about the companies that currently control that market share. You want to know their pricing formula, cost of equipment, and customer base (corporations, schools, sports teams, family reunions, etc.). The reason why this is so important to you is, that you want to create a unique edge that allows your business to attract more sales than your competitors. If you are going to sell t-shirts online, it is also important that you research the top online firms, by reviewing their websites. I recommend you signup for their emails, so you can learn about their marketing strategy.

Therefore, before you begin to create your strategy for managing competition, creating a competitors map can be useful. A competitors map is an analytical tool that organizes information on key points of your direct competitors. See the example below.

Adaptation of the Competitors Map

By creating this map, you will have a clear understanding of the brick and mortar locations in your area, but also use it to understand online competition. You may also want to become a customer of your competitor. This will allow you to evaluate customer service, quality of the product, pricing, and other features.

As you are focusing on understanding competitors, you must determine how your business will fit within your industry. When you conduct your analysis, you may determine a competitive advantage on products, services, or pricing. However, without conducting some analysis you will not identify areas where you are weak, and most importantly, areas where you are strong. When completing your competitors map, I recommend you use the following chart as a guide to conduct your analysis. Compare your company against two other leading competitors in your market. Use the words: Good, Better, or Best in your analysis.

	Your Business	Company A	Company B
Image			
Location			
Layout			
Suppliers			
Parking			
Product			
Services			
Pricing			
Sales			
Advertising			

Now, let's examine some of the areas that appeared on the analysis chart. When looking at the image of a business, how do customers perceive your reputation and the physical appearance of your location? When looking at your location, is the business in a convenient area? How is parking and visibility for your customers? When looking at the atmosphere, what happens when customers enter your facility? How does it make them feel? When looking at the price of your products, do customers believe the price is appropriate for the product or service they receive? When a customer visits your establishment, looking for a product, how easy is it to locate?

After you have conducted a solid competitor's analysis you can now create a solid strategic plan for your business. Your competitors map may show you that there are no competitors within a 20-mile radius, or there is a competitor every mile within your area. You may determine that creating an online store on Etsy, Amazon or eBay is your best alternative.

A strategic plan helps small business owners define their competitive advantage by analyzing the business environment, competitors, and drafting an appropriate strategy. Therefore, when you think about your strategic plan, use the following six-step process. (1) formulate your mission statement (2) complete an environmental analysis (3) define your competitive advantage (4) analyze your strategic alternative (5) set goals and strategies and (6) set up a control system.

Let's begin with the mission statement. The mission statement answers one simple question, what business am I in? When you create a specific purpose, scope, and direction for your business, you are communicating with your customers and employees what your business will provide, and how it will be provided. This mission statement is the foundation for building your marketing strategy, goals, and objectives. Therefore, it is important to note, that when a firm does not have a mission statement, the values and beliefs may be interpreted based on the actions of the owners or other key employees.

Thus, when you think about your mission, remember three important terms. These terms are, simplify, self-igniting, and value alignment. Let's take a look at all three. When you look at the word simplify, you ensure your mission statement is 25 words or less. Simplifying the message allows everyone to understand and articulate it. Self-igniting allows you to talk about you and your business for the benefit of all stakeholders. Finally, value alignment is important, because the impact of value alignment goes beyond money. It determines how well your mission and vision align with your values.

Google several firms to see what their mission statement is. I have provided some examples for you. Kickstarter's mission statement is "to help bring creative projects to life". The American Heart Association's mission statement is "to build healthier lives, free of cardiovascular diseases and stroke. Warby Parker's mission statement is to offer designer eyewear at a revolutionary price while leading the way for socially conscious businesses. The mission statement for my company, RBH Professional Development Institute, is to help people tap into their leadership skills, identify their gifts, and create a meaningful purpose for life. Notice, these mission statements are simple, self-igniting, and value-aligned.

The next area that is important for your competitive advantage is conducting an environmental analysis. The environmental analysis allows you to understand what is going on within any sector that affects the business externally or internally. This analysis allows you to adapt to change. One of my favorite methods for analysis involves using the Swot Analysis approach. A swot analysis allows you to identify the strengths, weaknesses, threats, and opportunities associated with your business.

EXTERNAL ANALYSIS

When you think about a SWOT analysis, note the external analysis focuses on opportunities and threats to the business. These opportunities and threats are outside your control. When you think of opportunities they are positive alternatives that support your mission and vision. Your task as a small business owner is to pursue the best opportunities for your business.

When you think about threats, these are obstacles to achieving the company's mission. Threats are events that you have no control over. Some threats are pandemics, changes in interest rates, government regulations, or a new competitor. To manage threats effectively, small business owners need to scan the following areas: the economy, legal, sociocultural, technology, and competitive environments.

Economy

As a small business owner, what do I need to know about the economy that can impact my target market? Some economic issues to consider include the unemployment rate, interest rates, tax rates within your community, and taxes for states where you want to operate your business. If I am expanding the business globally, what do I need to know about other nations related to their economies and taxes?

Legal

When reviewing legal issues, small business owners need to understand federal and state laws. For example, marijuana has been legalized in several states, but not recognized in all states. If this is the business you wish to specialize in understanding the laws for that state would be critical. Another important legal change is paying sales tax. In South Dakota vs. Wayfair, the Supreme Court ruled that states could collect Sales Tax for products sold beyond their borders. Depending on your product line, and growth strategies, this can have a huge impact on your business.

Sociocultural

As a small business owner, it is important to understand what society desires as they move from one cycle of life to the next. Obtaining this information can help you define your competitive advantage. For example, the generation that is using Facebook has changed. Generation Z is now on Tik Tok or using Twitter. As a business owner, it will be important to communicate a message for each group. This is one reason why I love teaching college students, they keep me up on the current trends.

Technology

Technology allows for the business to use scientific knowledge for practical purposes. Mobile apps such as Paypal and Square allow customers to sell their products at trade shows, fairs, and book events. Vlogs allow business owners to promote their business, tell a story, or stay connected to their customers. Technology opens the door and allows your business to stay competitive.

Competition

Competitors are forces within your marketplace. You must not only compete with them, you must also predict their moves. A good example is when airlines began charging for carry on luggage. After one airline made this move others followed. We often see this example, when a business drops their price, and they wait to see if the other businesses in the market place will do the same. In my managerial economics course, we call this game theory. This theory forces you to sit in your competitor's seat, and view competition through their eyes.

Internal Analysis

The internal analysis assesses the strengths and weaknesses of your company. The analysis will help you understand what you do well and areas that need improvement. These are areas where you will have some control. You can also use internal analysis to match the strength of your organization with opportunities. You must also understand that the weaknesses of the organization will connect to threats that may harm your business' existence. Therefore, when you conduct your internal analysis and are looking to analyze any potential problems, I recommend you evaluate the following:

- Review the colors and images you use for the marketing of your organization. Review your website, podcasts, and videos to determine if your message is consistent.

- Identify the business principles that matter to you. Evaluate if you see these principles listed on your website, business cards, brochures, etc.

- Survey customers to see how they feel about your product or service.

- Review your relationships with key suppliers.

- Use mystery shoppers in your business, so they can provide objective feedback about your products or services.

- Have a conversation with newly hired employees, to see how they feel about your organization or product. Check to see if they understand your principles.

STRATEGIC ALTERNATIVES

Another area that I want to focus on involves analyzing strategic alternatives for your business. While monitoring your competitive advantage, you may find opportunities exist based on mistakes made by your competitors. You may see an expansion of your product based on technology improvements. You may find that a pivot in your strategy supports growth. One of the best examples I can provide are individuals who discovered how to sell PPE equipment during the pandemic. These small business owners were able to pivot. The analysis of their strategic alternatives, helped them survive during tough economic times.

GOALS AND CONTROLS

Creating goals for your business does not mean issues will not surface. The plans you create ensure that you have a process in place that allows you a chance for survival. Attaching effective strategies to your goals and plans are key. Because businesses face so many negative forces, Control procedures are needed. Controls provide information that allows you to start the process over again.

One step I recommend is reviewing your business goals, to see if they still line up with your mission. Determine if you need new goals or if the time frame for those goals needs modification. I recommend you apply the smart principle.

Often when we hear about the smart principle, it is related to personal goals. In this example, you can apply the smart principle to your business goals. The smart principle stands for specific written goals that are measurable, attainable, realistic, and timely. These principles provide consistent control mechanisms, to measure organizational goals and adjust as needed.

By understanding competition, and the need for competitive analysis, SWOT analysis, and strategic goal planning, you can ensure that your business will manage the five forces of competition and remain competitive in the marketplace.

5

Characteristics and Competencies

One of the areas often overlooked by new business owners is a competency self-assessment of the business owner's experience, skills, and qualifications. You may be reading this and saying to yourself, "I know enough to get by" or "I got this under control." This may be true as you assess your current situation. However, for a new business owner, this is a very important assessment.

A review of competencies allows you to identify your skill, knowledge, and abilities as it relates to your business idea. This information allows you to evaluate your business behavior as it relates to determining how well you fit with the venture you are getting ready to launch.

Here's the thing, running a small business is challenging, and every person must know their strengths and weaknesses and how they stack up as it relates to the success of their business. As you begin to move forward with your business venture, it is important to evaluate your competency.

A self-assessment of your skills allows you to determine if you understand the basic key functions to run a business and have industry-specific knowledge. You are also able to evaluate your resource competencies, determination competencies, and opportunity competencies. The goal is to help the business owner identify areas that need strengthening. By examining yourself, you can identify your skills, compare yourself with others, and make the necessary adjustments to move forward.

Now, I want you to focus on what I have labeled as the 5 Ps of entrepreneur behavior. The five P's are passion, perseverance, promotion, planning, and professionalism. Let's begin with passion. Passion is an intensive feeling you have as an entrepreneur towards your business idea. Passion is the fire that ignites your effort in moving the idea forward. Passion is displayed in several ways: (a) being focused on the business, (b) absorbed by the concerns of the business, and (c) looking at roadblocks as opportunities.

Next, let's look at perseverance. Perseverance connects to optimism, which is the ability to stick with an idea or activity when success is not immediately seen. Perseverance is probably the most important characteristic for the entrepreneur, because when you persevere you push yourself, towards success. You do not let the words of naysayers stop you. As a matter of fact, you use that as fuel. You believe you have a product or service that will help the community. When you persevere, you know that failure is not fatal, it is a learning experience.

Promotion, as a competency, requires that the business owner, utilize two schools of thought as it relates to business success. The first school of thought requires the business owner, to develop a promotion-focused mentality. This will allow the business owner to focus on opportunities that maximize business gains. The second school of thought requires the business owner to develop a prevention-focused mentality, where the business owner identifies risks that can harm the business.

Planning for a business is very important, and it is important to recognize that there is more than one way to plan for business success. Let's discuss a few. One strategy focuses on a comprehensive strategy for your business. When using this strategy, the business owner develops a long-term plan for the business, one that he is satisfied and comfortable with.

Another approach is the opportunistic method. Business owners start with a goal and look for opportunities that support the achievement of that goal. Once they have identified a good opportunity, they will pursue it.

Another type of planner is a critical thinking business planner. This planner identifies the most important aspects of the business first and then acts on these issues. The critical thinking planner will consider additional items as they are needed.

Reactive business owners rely on cues from the business environment, to determine the path forward. This is a short-term approach to planning. This method allows the business owner to handle short term concerns but does not consider long term solutions.

The last planning method I want to discuss is the Habit-based planner. Habit based planners focus on routines. They allow their routines to dictate their business decisions. They follow the same path they were using the day before. This approach does not allow them to react to market conditions and other changes in the business environment. They believe a routine approach is the best method for business success.

The final P we will discuss is professionalism. As a small business owner, it is important to understand how professionalism can separate you from your competitors. One standard business practice that supports this effort, is for entrepreneurs to provide a particular product or service, above average. This product or service might be the hallmark of your operation. For example, when I think about the Ruth Chris steakhouse, they are recognized for providing world-class steaks, as a signature entrée on their menu. Though they provide other entrees, steaks are the hallmark of their success and they serve it with the highest dignity and professionalism.

Being average is often labeled as the industry standard. For many business professionals, this is not acceptable. However, the great part about being in business is, that you get a chance to make that choice. So let's stop here and examine and define the three levels of business professionalism. This gives you the chance to choose what level your business will provide.

The three levels of business professionalism are, the expert business professional, the specialized business professional, and the minimalized business professional. A firm that has identified being an expert, as part of its business model, is focused on exceeding industry standards. Being average is considered failing among this group. They may often highlight this point in their advertising.

Another level that firms define themselves as, is specialized business professionals. Among this level, owners tend to be more passionate about several of the business functions, such as sales, operations, or accounting. The third level is the minimalized business professional. At this level none of the aspects of the business support industry standards. The owner focuses on providing every product or service in the most simple manner.

If you notice, from the information shared in this chapter, these behaviors are useful in business and in life. The key to understanding professionalism is recognizing that the type of professional service you deliver, takes place during all phases of your business. Therefore, it is important for you to select your level of professionalism and establish it at the beginning of your endeavor. In coaching business clients, I often say to them, start the process the way you want it to end.

As I conclude this chapter, I have an assessment of the 5 P's for you to complete, which examines your psychology as a business owner, along with a competency self-assessment. These assessments are designed to will help you identify the strengths and weaknesses of your business model, identify what statements match your belief or approach, and help you identify your behaviors towards entrepreneurship. Examine the following questions, and determine how strongly you agree or disagree with the statement. Place a checkmark in the appropriate box. Your results may give you great insight about your business mindset.

	Strongly Agree				Strongly Disagree
	1	2	3	4	5
I am excited to be starting a new business.					
Owning my own business is more important than spending time with my family.					
I really enjoy nurturing a new business through its emerging success.					
Sometimes, I have a hard time staying motivated.					
I tend to give up when things become difficult.					
I enjoy solving problems.					
I enjoy using my creative skills.					
I believe in myself and my abilities.					
I usually compare myself to others.					
I am affected by what other people think.					
I have a hard time staying focused.					
I have a hard time asking for help.					
I start things but rarely finish them.					

Use the same ranking system in this section, as above. 1 being that you strongly agree, through 5 that you strongly disagree.

Rank 1-5	
	I am most comfortable when I plan for everything.
	I am always looking for the next big thing.
	Whatever happens, I stick to my original plan.
	I feel best when everything I do is done in the best way possible.
	I think it is important to be recognized for doing things well.
	Making money is the most important thing.
	I am a competitive person.
	I believe it is more important to get the job done, than to try and make it perfect.
	I believe that average is good enough.
	I don't give up until I win.
	The satisfaction of my customer is the most important thing.

In this section, you want to focus on your business acumen for running your business. The following checklist will help you determine your business-related expertise or competence. The purpose is to help you identify where you are strong, and showcase areas where you will improve your knowledge and skills.

Here are examples that define the following key business competencies for entrepreneurship.

- **Key business function** – defines activities common for all businesses such as sales, operation, accounting, finance, and human resources.

- **Industry-specific knowledge** – describes the

knowledge, skill, and activities specific to your particular industry.

- **Resource Competencie**s – the skill of the business owner at finding expendable components necessary for the operation of the business, such as information, location, financing, raw materials, and expertise.

- **Determination competencies** – skills identified with the focus required to bring a business into existence.

- **Opportunity competencie**s – skills necessary to identify elements of the business environment that can lead to a profitable and sustainable business.

Take the following assessment and determine your level of competence in these key areas. Place a check in the box that best fits your current level.

	Needs Development	Needs Refinement	Competent	Excellent
Key Business Functions				
Sales				
Operation				
Accounting				
Human Resources				
Finance				
Industry-Specific Skills				
Expertise				
Skill				
Market Knowledge				
Ability to see opportunities				

In this section of the competency assessment, you want to focus on your personal knowledge of key business areas. I used this section to review what I knew about operations and sales. I also used this section to review what I knew about leadership training, public speaking, coaching and book publishing.

Resource Competencies				
Business information				
Business financing				
Logistics				
Raw Material sourcing				
Support Personnel				
Determination Competencies				
Ability to manage time				
Business focus and attention				
Ability to sustain relationships				
Ability to act or make a decision				
Opportunity Competencies				
Finding new opportunities				
Creating new ideas				
Exploring new innovations				

In this section you want to focus on what you know about logistics and also assess your skill sets for building key business relationships. I used this section to focus on my skills working with suppliers, banks, and my willingness to make key business decisions for the organization.

In this chapter, we focused our attention on you as the business owner by discussing the psychology of being an entrepreneur. The presence of certain skills makes a huge difference when looking at who will start a business, from those who will not. Now that you have taken both the psychological test, as well as the competency skills assessment, let's evaluate what you have learned.

As you evaluate yourself, keep an open mind about your knowledge, skills, and abilities. All of the information will be useful in helping you when you start your business.

What did you learn about your business mindset?

_____

_____

_____

_____

_____

What do you believe were your core strengths?

_____

_____

_____

_____

What areas did you discover that you need improvement in?

_____

_____

_____

_____

_____

How will this assessment help you, moving forward?

_____

_____

_____

_____

_____

6

Credit

Finding the money to start or grow your business is one of the greatest challenges a business owner will encounter. New business owners often have to rely on their personal resources, as lenders often do not want to take a chance on a new business. We will revisit and take a deeper dive into this challenge in a later segment. However, people who want to start a business often find ways to get it done.

In this chapter we want to focus on understanding financing, debt capital, credit, expenses, and cash resources, so you can determine what is the best option for your business. For all new business owners, often the main source of startup capital is coming from your resources. This may include your credit cards, savings account, retirement savings, or a home equity loan. In each case, the business owner (you) has to determine if using your resources to start your business is worth the risk. No one can answer this question, but you.

Therefore, if you are going to start with your resources, you want to ask yourself some important questions:

1. How much do I want to invest?

2. Am I getting ready to retire?

3. How will my spouse or significant other respond?

4. Do I have an emergency savings account to handle my expenses?

5. Is this the business venture I want to pursue?

By answering these questions at the beginning, you can begin to evaluate your strategies related to funding and be open when attempting to understand and identify your startup expenses. This will prepare you for the growth phase, where you will understand the need to identify resources and focus on creating a constant flow of capital assets that promote growth and stability.

Therefore, before we talk about expenses and financing, it is important to look at the funding of your business as equity. Equity includes personal equity (owner's equity), debt capital, and gift capital. Business financing comes from personal funds, family and friends, credit cards, trade credit, banks, credit unions, angel investors, community-based financiers, stock sales, and venture capitalists. The key for you at the startup phase and growth phase is to identify the best resource that supports your business.

As a new business owner, it is important to know that funding your business takes planning. It also requires research of funding opportunities and improvements in your negotiation skills. If you are afraid of people, now is the time to become comfortable when you are talking to strangers. Finally, in this phase, new business owners get discouraged. This is what I consider "The make or break phase" where you must be committed to the business while waiting on your necessary funding source.

Now let's take a look at your expenses. Expenses will vary based on the business type, location, state, etc. Some of your expenses will be monthly, and some will be part of your startup costs. Therefore, your first goal is to identify all of your expenses by making a list.

Some common startup costs include office space, equipment, supplies, utilities, licenses, permits, insurance, legal, accounting, inventory, employee salaries, advertising, market research, printed materials, website, business registration fees, and any other miscellaneous expenses. After you have created your list, you can estimate how much these startup expenses will cost. As a guide, please take a look at the following startup expense worksheets that have been provided for you. You can recreate these documents in Microsoft Excel.

Startup Expenses

Sources of Capital

Owners' Investment (name and percent ownership)

    Your name and percent ownership

    Other investor

    Other investor   –

    Total Investment

    Bank Loans

    Bank 1

    Bank 2

    Total Bank Loans

Startup Expenses

Real Estate Expenses

Purchase

Construction

Remodeling

Other

Total Real Estate Expenses

Leasehold Improvements

Item 1

Item 2

Total Leasehold Improvements

Capital Equipment List

Furniture

Equipment

Fixtures

Machinery

Other

Total Capital Equipment

Admin Expenses

Rent & Related Costs

Utility deposits

Legal and accounting fees

Prepaid insurance

Pre-opening salaries

Other

Total Admin Expenses

Opening Inventory

Category 1

Category 2

Total Inventory

<u>Advertising Expenses</u>

Advertising

Signage

Printing

Travel/entertainment

Other categories

Total Advertising Expenses

<u>Other Expenses</u>

Other expense 1

Other expense 2

Total Other Expenses

    Reserved for Contingencies

<u>Working Capital</u>

Owners' and other investments

Bank loans

Other loans

Total Source of Funds

Total Startup Expenses

One of the strategies I use is, to identify my monthly costs after the initial startup costs are covered. It is also important for all business owners to understand the federal, state, and local tax laws as it relates to starting their business. You will find that there are some expenses, that all business owners face.

I promised that we would delve a little deeper into funding, so here we go. As we said earlier, many entrepreneurs are forced to look into their own pockets for the cash to start a business. This, as I have stated, is because banks and other investors often do not want to gamble on a business that has no history or established track record. As we face this fact, it is now time for us to look at some alternative methods of funding for your business. Bootstrapping is one of those methods. Bootstrapping is a process where you use low cost or free techniques to minimize your cost of doing business. Plainly stated, bootstrapping is saving money. There are some good reasons for bootstrapping, and they are as follows:

- External equity capital is normally not available.

- Owners often do not want to share ownership of their new business.

- Owners would like to leave their present employer to become their own boss.

Thus, bootstrapping has become a common method for new business startups. The key issue when thinking about bootstrapping is, how can I use this method to start and grow the business. Now I would like to share information on key business areas, where you can successfully apply your bootstrapping methods. The first area that I want to discuss is how you can use bootstrapping to minimize overhead. When we look at minimizing overhead, the key is to identify areas where you can reduce costs. Here are some examples for reducing overhead expenses:

- Instead of purchasing Microsoft Office Professional for $450.00 use Google docs for business, which averages about $10 per month.

- Instead of opening up a storefront for your business, create a virtual storefront using platforms such as eBay, Amazon, or Shopify.

- Use a business incubator. Business incubators offer office space and services at a lower cost compared to renting office space.

- Find a business office co-op. These establishments rent individual offices, but share common space and equipment which includes copiers and administrative support. Doctors, lawyers, and insurance agents utilize these office setups.

- Use coworking spaces – Coworking spaces allow you to rent office space by the day, week, or month. These locations also have conference rooms, business lounges, and other amenities.

Operating costs are often a huge expense for a business. After you determine your office location, you often have to focus on other types of business expenses. These expenses can include inventory, insurance, licensing, and telephone service. Listed below are examples for reducing other overhead expenses:

- Outsource the production of your service or product. When you outsource the production, you do not have to stock the raw materials. Also, you do not have to pay for full-time employees, manage payroll taxes, and other required employee benefits.

- Think about subcontracting part of your business that is not a core competency. For example, if you are a carpenter, you may want to subcontract the painting and landscaping part of your business, but not the main service. You are still able to provide the service, but you have reduced the overhead.

- Investigate the renting of time, as it relates to business equipment. If you are starting a screen-printing business, and cannot afford the equipment, negotiate a rental agreement with a local screen-printer. This is helpful when you know how to produce your product.

- Rent equipment. If you are starting a catering business and you land a contract for a corporate event, rent a portable cooker for the event. As you begin to grow the business, you can determine if this is the equipment you should purchase.

- Seek trade credit terms with key suppliers.

- Use teleconferencing for meetings, to reduce travel expenses.

- Work from home. Starting your business in your home is probably the most widely accepted method. You can set up an internet and telephone service with one provider.

Another method for bootstrapping is understanding how to minimize employee costs to get the optimum value for your product or service. Here are some examples to consider:

- Hire contractors to complete a task. You can hire contractors for a month, three months, or a year. Contractors can handle tasks such as web creation, sales reports, production, or working on a catering job.

- Network with a community college and hire interns who are motivated to gain experience, and are willing to work for a lower salary.

- Use overtime if it is feasible. Paying your current employees overtime, can be cheaper than hiring a new employee. In the case of overtime, it will be important to consider new rules regarding overtime pay for white-collar employees.

The final area associated with bootstrapping that I want to

cover is, reducing your marketing costs. When you are starting and growing your business, you must maximize your resources. This will ensure that your marketing efforts are leading to increases in revenue. Learning how to leverage free ink and free advertising is the way to get the biggest bang for your buck. Consider the following examples:

- Word of mouth – This is the best marketing technique.

- Use customers to promote your product, by having them share their experience.

- Offer discounts for customers who recommend your business.

- Social Media – Create followers on your social media websites, and return the favor by following them. This will increase your exposure and add to your customer base.

- Utilize press releases. Reporters are always looking for local news. A well-designed press kit about your business can provide the local news team with a filler story.

- Embrace public speaking – Present a 10 or 15 minute speech about your business to the local Rotary Club, Kiwanis Club, Toastmasters Club, or Chamber of Commerce. This can also be used as a networking tool.

- Donate your service or product to noteworthy groups. If you own a restaurant, offer some free food to a nonprofit. Or, donate products to the local news station to promote fundraising goals.

The next method that I want to cover related to funding your business is crowdfunding. Crowdfunding can be an effective way to raise awareness about your business idea. In a study published by the National Federation of Independent Business, online nonbank lenders such as Kabbage and Kickstarter have become viable alternatives. These online platforms cater to financing loans under $250,000. This alternative is good for businesses that require fewer start-up assets. It will be important to understand the laws especially if you are seeking donations from other countries. This is important as laws vary by country.

The next step in this process is to set a goal for the amount of money you would like to raise over a period of time. Invite friends, family members, and donors to pledge funds on crowdfunding sites. Sites such as Kickstarter and Indiegogo have raised significant funds for items such as 3D printed pens or smartwatches as part of a fundraising campaign. With crowdfunding, it is important to remember that the investor receives a reward for their investment. Please remember to review the rules of the crowdfunding provider.

Another way to fund your business is for the business owner to sell shares in their company. Individuals who buy ownership in a firm are considered outside equity investors. It is important to note, that ownership in a business can only be sold to a partnership, corporation, or limited liability company (LLC).

The next area I want to focus on, as it relates to funding your business, is through debt financing. Debt financing is provided through commercial banks, SBA loans, economic development agencies, incubators, leasing companies, personal credit cards, small business investment companies, business credit cards, lines of credit, factoring of receivables, and suppliers. Small business owners will use debt financing at the startup phase, growth phase, financing for operations phase, or exit phase of the business.

Debt financing is the claim on the value of assets owned by the business. Secured debt provides a lender the right to seize specific assets if the debt is not repaid. Unsecured debt does not allow the lender to seize assets. The lender will have to sue the business to collect the unpaid unsecured debt.

The final area I want to discuss is gift financing. Gift capital is normally available for businesses that have several successful years of operation. The business is also meeting a societal goal, and the gifts are funded through the government or private foundations.

As we wrap up this final segment on funding, you must now do some reflection and soul searching. The first order of business is to determine your start-up costs and determine how much of your own resources, if any, you will use to invest in your business. You must also assess other ways to raise your needed funds. You must allocate an amount, yet not lose sight of the other important responsibilities in your life.

For example, a spouse or significant other, small children, children in college, medical issues, and retirement can all be impacted by your decision. Establishing the proper balance between your business and personal life will be crucial. Once you have closed the chapter on these issues, it is now time for the next important step, banking.

One of the first steps a small business owner completes is opening up a business checking account. A business checking account allows you to establish a relationship with a bank. The bank can provide you with a business debit card, that allows you a way to manage expenses until you can establish credit in the business's name.

Many entrepreneurs use their equity (personal credit cards) at the beginning of the startup phase. However, the startup phase can be risky, when you mix personal expenses with your business expenses. It is important to document your business expenses on your credit cards and keep the receipts. After you have been in business for several months, up to a year, you can begin to apply for a credit card through your bank. You may consider providers such as American Express, which is my personal favorite. Your banking relationship will pay dividends for you over the long haul.

7

Feasibility of a Business Idea

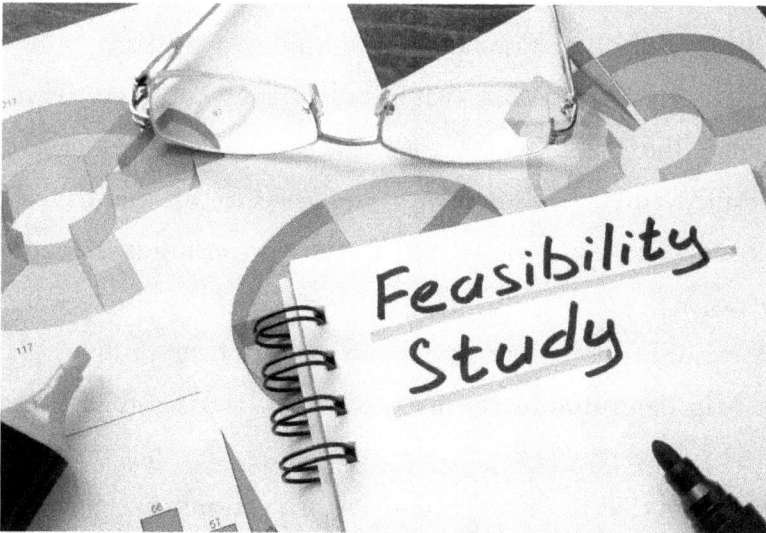

In the past, traditional business plans have been the normal channel for business startups. The problem that some business owners have faced is, believing they can identify and solve all problems a business encounters, by using their business plan. However, business plans, are just that, business plans. They are not designed to react to real-world changes and market uncertainties. In order to create a sustainable business model or idea, owners use a variety of methods. Some involve screening of the business idea, to test its viability. The idea for the business might be new in the United States, but someone in England has come up with the same idea.

Businesses are also using a new concept, entitled lean startup. The focus of this concept is to get the product in the hands of consumers as quickly as possible. Here, the business uses an academic term entitled, build-measure-learn. The concept is to turn your idea into something fast, obtain feedback on what is working, and pivot based on what you have learned.

There is another tool that can help new business owners evaluate the feasibility of their ideas. This tool is called a feasibility study. This process is designed to test the feasibility of your idea, by conducting a study or using a screening process.

A feasibility study can assess part, or all of the business plan, and help determine if the idea will work. A feasibility study focuses on several key areas, including the business idea, product/service, industry, financial projections, and plans for future action. Within these areas, the study digs deeper into the description of the business, product benefits, limitations, market feasibility, market potential, technical feasibility, raw materials, financials, business founders, and next steps. Now we will discuss the key components of a feasibility study.

Business Description

The first area we will discuss is the description of the business idea, based on its industry affiliation. When describing the feasibility of your idea, it is important to describe the business you want to be in and eliminate models that do not make sense.

Market Feasibility

The next area of the feasibility study looks at market feasibility. In this section, you will describe the industry, and estimate the future direction of that industry. You do not want to create a product for an industry in decline, unless you truly believe your idea will revive the industry. It will also be important for you to determine the level of competitiveness that exists within the industry. Finally, determine how you will price your product or service.

Market Potential

The third area focuses on market potential. Here you will determine whether your product is to be sold into a commodity market or a differentiated market. You will examine emerging, niche, or segmented market opportunities. Is the product for women, men, youth, etc. When looking at market potential, you will identify the demand and usage trends for your particular market. You will evaluate your market share and estimate your revenue. Finally, project your sales under various scenarios.

Technology

The fourth area of the feasibility study looks at the impact of technology. Here you want to determine what is needed for your facility. It will be important to review technology providers for your website or e-commerce platform. Are there other environmental concerns? You also want to understand your access to raw materials, transportation, labor, and production.

Raw Materials

The fifth area of the study is looking at the raw materials needed for your product or service. You want to estimate the amount of raw material needed. You want to identify any additional inputs related to producing the product. This can include labor and skills. Most importantly, you want to determine the current and future access to raw materials. For example, if you are importing the raw materials, what happens if government leadership changes? What happens if there is a natural disaster.

Financials

The sixth area of the study focuses on the financials. It is important here to estimate working capital needs. You want to identify startup capital needs. Capital for equipment, facilities, and inventory. You also want to create a contingency plan for your capital needs, to ensure that you can fund the first few years of your business.

Equity and Credit

The seventh area of your feasibility study focuses on equity and credit. Here it is important to begin by identifying equity and alternative sources for capital. You may begin with your personal funds. Is that going to be enough? You will want to list family members, angel investors, venture capitalists, and others who can help fund your new business venture. Finally, in this area, you want to create an estimated budget and benchmark industry averages.

Organizational Structure

In the eight area of the feasibility study, you will focus on the organizational structure. In this section, you will identify the proposed legal structure for your business. You must determine if you want to be a sole proprietor, S corporation, Limited Liability Corporation, Partnership, or if your state allows Certified B corporations. As you are determining the structure, identify potential managers, and other key personnel.

Management

The final area in the feasibility study identifies who will lead the project. Do the founders have the drive required to take the project through to completion. Will everyone associated with the business have the skills and knowledge? After your feasibility study is complete, you must determine whether a viable business opportunity exists. If the answer is yes, you should produce a business plan or continue further research.

8

Your Business Plan

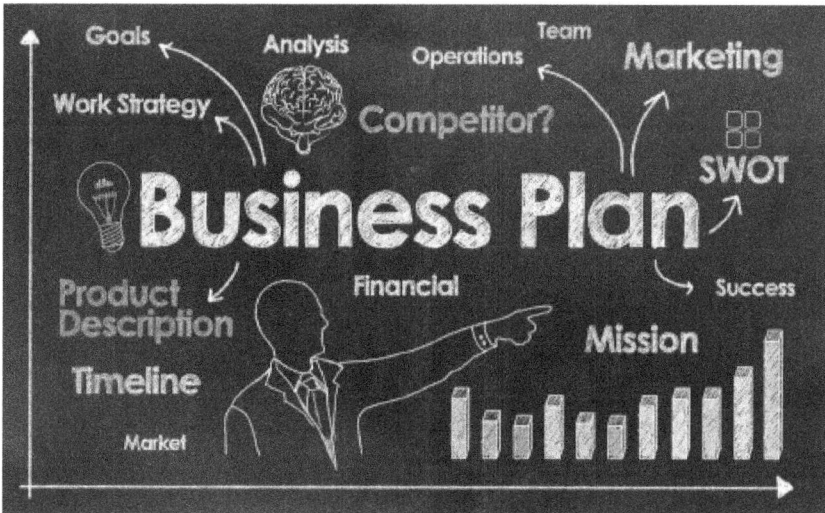

In the previous chapters, we have focused on understanding the importance of credit, concept, competition, customers, competencies, and the feasibility study for your business. All areas are important when starting a business. In this chapter, we are going to focus on the business plan itself.

In today's business environment, a business plan is one of a small business owner's most crucial business documents. No company can expect to articulate its goals and secure financing without a well-conceived, and well-presented, plan. This convincing plan helps others seriously look at the goals of your business.

The purpose of developing a business plan is, to have a successful business. When creating a business plan, include the long-term needs of your business and devise strategies that enhance the overall performance of your company. A business plan is a living document that describes your concept, market, business goals, major characteristics, and strategies for turning your concept into a reality.

When you think about your business plan, it is important to think about the audience who will review the plan. One strategy I recommend is the creation of several plans, depending on the audience. When you understand your intended audience, you can identify their needs. For example, if you are seeking support from family and friends, some of their concerns might include the use of the funds, stability of your firm, and the timeline for returning their investment.

If your business plan is for angel investors, some of their concerns will include, the product or service market, growth, team, and return on investment. If the plan is for potential partners, they will be concerned about the fit between the firms, benefits, comparative advantage, and intellectual property rights. If the business plan is for bankers, they will be concerned about cash flow, cash cycle, assets, collateral, and long-term prospects.

You may also want to take advantage of a current popular strategy called the lean business model, where you place your product or service in the market, obtain customer feedback, and modify your strategy accordingly. This lean business model will focus on your business pitch, business model canvas, and your financials. The important concept to remember is understanding your intended audience, and the requirements you will need to convey your idea.

Now, I would like to discuss the key components of a classic business plan. As mentioned earlier, a business plan is a blueprint for your business that tells a story about your product, service, or market potential. It helps bankers, potential partners, and other investors understand your strategy and plan for success.

Your business plan will be lengthy and will change as the needs for your business change. We will discuss two types of business plans which are, formal or informal. Listed below is a summary of what should be included in a formal business plan.

Executive summary

This is a key component of the business plan. It is an overview of the business problem, product, market, team, competitive advantage, and financial summary projections.

The executive summary will spell out the goals of your business plan.

Company Overview.

The next area of the plan is the company overview. In this section, you will provide information about your business, such as how and when it was started. This section will also include the mission statement, business model, strategy, and any strategic relationships. You may want to talk about the legal structure of the business and any other administrative issues.

Business Offering.

In this section, you share information about your products or services. You will also share information on why you are in business. You can also use this section to identify the problem, or need, that this business offering fills.

If you sell a product, define whether you are the producer, distributor, or retailer of the product. Define your manufacturing process, inventory, or fulfillment services. If you provide a business service, define your service. If you have future products or services, you can also share that information with your audience in this section.

Marketing Plan.

The fourth area of the plan covers your marketing plan and marketing analysis. You begin this section by providing information on your marketing analysis, customers, advertising, and public relations. When sharing information about your customers, identify who they are, and how you will find them.

You may want to highlight why your business will be successful, making the connection to your market research of the industry. You will also share information on the marketing channels included in your business model canvas. This is a very important section of your business plan because it helps your audience understand who will buy your product or service.

Marketing Strategy.

The fifth area outlines your marketing strategy. When you think about your marketing strategy it should focus on three areas. The first part of the strategy outlines the overall strategy your firm will pursue. Here you can include information on differentiation, cost, or focus.

The second part of the marketing strategy identifies how you will apply the strategy to secure customers. In this section, you include information on how sales will be achieved. This area may include information on your promotional or distribution efforts.

The last step highlights how you protect your firm from competition. Competitors are not generally trying to give up their market share. Therefore in this section provide a long-term strategy on how you will hold off competition. This can include information on future products, or list strategies that play against the weaknesses of your competitors.

Management

The sixth area of the plan focuses on you and your organization. This area is also very critical, especially if you are writing a business plan for angel investors or bankers. Here you want to explain your background and the background of your executives and managers. You want to talk about their skills, and how those skills will help you meet your goals. You want to talk about your accomplishments and not just experience. You want to impress the reader.

As you talk about your accomplishments, do not limit yourself to just business, talk about social accomplishments, associations to civic organizations, and community involvement. Those activities may be important to the reader. Also, if you have a major relationship with an organization, individual, or team, share that information. If you have a board of directors or a team of advisors, list them here. The goal is to help the reader gain confidence in you and your team.

Financial Summary

The Seventh area of the business plan provides a financial summary. You can include projected profit and loss statements, your balance sheet, and cash flow statements for three years. These are important because they forecast the future. In this section, you can also include an exit summary. This shows your plans for the future.

With some business plans, you may want to include your IPO listing, information on selling the business to family members, franchising, etc. The final area in this section outlines your funding request. Here is where you ask for the funding. Therefore, you want to be as precise as you can, and most importantly do not overstate sales or profits.

At the end of this section is the Appendix. In the Appendix section of the plan, you can include other supporting documentation. Some examples include resumes, bios. letters of commitment, press releases, price lists, and results of marketing surveys.

The Informal Plan

The next area outlines the informal business plan. If you are not seeking angel investors or funding from banks, create a simple plan. A simple business plan is helpful when you want to jump into the marketplace with your product or service. An informal plan can help you define your goals, sales strategy, and market potential. Listed below are sections to include in your informal plan.

Company Description

The first section should include your company description and mission statement. Describe your business, legal structure, and the products and services you will provide. You can also include a description of your management team, detailing each person's job duties and responsibilities.

Market

The second area of this plan should include information on your potential market. In this section, talk about the customers you will serve and how they will utilize your product or service. This section allows you to define the demographics, location, buying patterns, and age of your customers. This section helps to reinforce to your reader, that you have identified your customer.

Competition

The third section of this plan provides an overview of the competition. Every business must identify their competitors. Therefore, list current or potential competitors, and identify their strengths and weaknesses. You can find this information by checking out their websites, blogs, and visiting their locations if one exists in your area.

Marketing Strategy

The fourth section of the plan focuses on your marketing strategy. In this section, you will describe how you will promote your business. As part of the marketing strategy, you want to identify what differentiates your product from your rival's. Also, determine how you will use social media campaigns, videos, promotional products, and other literature for advertisements. The goal is to determine how to get your product or service to customers.

Financial Summary

The fifth area of this plan includes a financial summary. Here, you will include your startup costs, your operating costs, and revenue estimates. When providing a financial overview, keep revenue and costs realistic. New business owners, should also prepare a cash flow statement so you understand how you will finance your organization. The cash flow statement also provides an overview of your cash flow position. One of the key struggles for new business owners is having enough cash at the beginning to finance the operation.

Pitch of the Presentation

The final area associated with your business plan is pitching your plan to potential investors. Depending on which plan you use, it may be important to present the plan to your investors. The pitch is built around a demo or prototype of your business. This presentation is labeled the pitch deck for your business. A business plan pitch allows you to provide an overview, followed by a question and answer session.

The key with your pitch is understanding that your listener is forming an idea about you and your business. Therefore, remember that the listener is looking for your passion for the business. They are also looking at your expertise as it relates to your business and the plan. Finally, they are looking at your professionalism, and how easy it will be working with you.

In creating your pitch presentation, it is important to focus on the mechanics of your presentation. Your pitch presentation should include the following: introduction, company purpose, business problem, solution, product, why now, market size, competition, management, financials, asking for funding, and your close.

9

Business Formation

In this section, I want to cover the legal framework for your business. This is important because you want to pick the best format that reduces your risks and provides the greatest benefits. The first order of business is selecting your legal name. When you think about your legal name, remember that this is your trade name or assumed name. This name will be registered in the states, in which, you operate your business.

When you select your name, think of something memorable that describes your product or service. If your goal is to use your name as the business name, be aware that if you sell the business, you will also be selling your name. Second, if it is a family business, you want a name that supports the family.

Take a moment and list some potential names for your business.

_____

_____

_____

_____

_____

_____

After you have selected your name, you will register the business name with your city, county, or state and apply for your federal identification number. The type of registration will be associated with the business format you select. Therefore your next step is selecting the right business type, and understanding the pros or cons of those available. Today there are several business types, and they are as follows: sole proprietorship, general partnership, limited partnership, C corporations S corporations, professional corporations, limited liability companies, and B Corporations depending on the state. Except for the sole proprietor, the business forms are all legal entities. Listed below are the features of all the previous listed business entities.

Let's begin by defining the sole proprietorship, and then move on to all of the other business entities. The sole proprietorship is the easiest form to create and easiest to close. It is owned and operated by one person. There are no legal requirements to establish a sole proprietorship. As you travel through the list, notice the features of each entity.

THE SOLE PROPRIETORSHIP

1. Most basic business format when starting a business.

2. Few legal requirements and restrictions.

3. You have the freedom to run the business as you choose.

4. Unlimited liability – As the business owner, you are personally liable for all debts. Please note, this liability can extend beyond the owner's investment in the business.

5. Resources may be limited. Resources are based on the owner's personal wealth.

PARTNERSHIP

A partnership is a legal entity of two or more people who co-own a business. For this type of business structure, owners should create a written document that defines the partnership.

One of the biggest advantages of a partnership is the pooling of management talent and the capital to create a product or service. Listed below are some other partnership features.

The Partnership Option

1. Involves consideration of legal issues as well as personal and managerial factors.

2. Partners should be honest, healthy, capable, and compatible.

3. Suggestions:

  • Test-drive the relationship. You want to make sure you will work well in business.

  • Create a combined vision for the business.

  • Prepare for the worst. It is important to prepare yourself for a financial setback or some other issue.

Rights and Duties of Partners

1. Partnership agreement – a document that states explicitly the rights and duties of partners (especially important with family members).

2. Joint and several liability – liability of each partner resulting from any of the partner's ability to legally bind the other partners.

Termination of a Partnership

1. Death, incapacity, or withdrawal of a partner ends the partnership.

2. Termination of the agreement requires liquidation or reorganization of the business.

3. May result in substantial losses to all partners, but may be necessary.

THE CORPORATION

The corporation is the most compacted business structure to form. A corporation is considered an autonomous entity that has the legal rights of a person, including the ability to sue and be sued. A corporation can own property and engage in business transactions.

1. Corporation – a business organization that exists as a legal entity and provides limited liability to its owners.

2. Legal entity – a business organization that is recognized by the law as having a separate legal existence.

3. The C corporation – ordinary corporation, taxed by the federal government as a separate legal entity.

The Corporate Charter

1. A document that establishes a corporation's existence.

2. Sometimes called articles of incorporation or certificate of incorporation.

3. Brief, per state law, and broad in its statement of the firm's powers.

4. Corporate bylaws outline the basic rules for ongoing formalities and decisions of a corporation, such as, the size of the board of directors, duties, and responsibilities of directors and officers, scheduling meetings of directors and shareholders, etc.

Rights and Status of Stockholders

1. Ownership evidenced by stock certificates (a document specifying the number of shares owned by a stockholder).

2. Pre-emptive right – the right of stockholders to buy new shares of stock before they are offered to the public.

Limited Liability of Stockholders- stockholder liability is restricted to the amount of money they invest in the business.

- Death or Withdrawal of Stockholders – ownership easily transferable.

- Maintain Corporate Status

1. Must hold annual meetings of both the shareholders and the board of directors.

2. Keep minutes to document the major decisions of shareholders and directors.

3. Maintain bank accounts separate from owners' bank accounts.

4. File separate income tax return for the business.

The Limited Partnership – a partnership with at least one general partner and one or more limited partners.

1. General partner – A partner who has unlimited liability and remains personally liable for debts of the business.

2. Limited partners – A partner who is not active in its management and has limited personal liability.

The Subchapter S Corporation

The Sub Chapter S corporation provides you with the limited-liability protection of a corporation, while allowing the tax advantages of a partnership. It avoids double taxation attached to corporations. The corporation files an informational tax return, but the income and expenses flow through to the shareholders based on the number of shares they own.

The S Corporation (Subchapter S Corporation)

1. Type of corporation that offers limited liability to its owners, but is taxed by the federal government as a partnership.

2. Must meet specific requirements

No more than 100 stockholders are allowed.

- All stockholders must be individuals or certain qualifying estates and trusts.

- Only one class of stock can be outstanding.

- Fiscally, the corporation must operate on a calendar-year basis.

- Shareholders may not include nonresident aliens.

The Limited Liability Company

1. Form of organization in which owners have limited liability and pay personal income taxes on business profits.

2. The major advantage is liability protection.

Usually the best choice for new businesses.

1. Ability to pass taxable income on to shareholders.

2. Easier to set up.

3. More flexible.

4. Significant tax advantages.

Better to use a C corporation if you want to:

1. Provide extensive fringe benefits to owners or employees.

2. Offer stock options to employees.

3. Go public or sell your equity.

4. Convert to a C corporation.

The Professional Corporation

1. Form of a corporation that shields owners from liability and is set up for individuals in certain professional practices.

2. Does not protect a practitioner from his/her negligence or malpractice.

Applies to a narrow range of enterprises.

1. Many states require this form of organization before a practice can operate.

The Nonprofit Corporation

1. Form of a corporation for enterprises established to serve civic, educational, charitable, or religious purposes but not for generation of profits.

2. Most become 501[c](3) organizations

3. IRS will not allow this option for an individual or partnership.

4. Organizational test – verification of whether a nonprofit organization is staying true to its stated purpose.

The B Corporation

1. B corporation—A form of corporation that creates a positive social or environmental impact, while maintaining high standards of transparency and accountability.

2. Strategic alliance—An organizational relationship that links two or more independent business entities in a common endeavor.

10

Business Financials

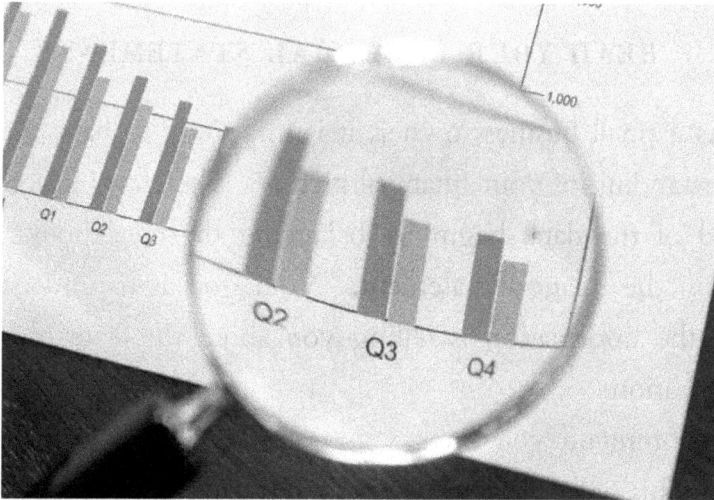

When it comes to understanding finances, small business owners can be divided into two categories. They are either fascinated by financial reports or scared to death.

Understanding your finances is very important because, as the decision-maker, your financial picture represents your business decisions. Therefore, when you think about financial data, know that it is not magical or mysterious, it is just the plain facts.

If you decide to advertise on Facebook and Twitter, there is a monthly cost for that advertising. If you projected sales for a particular quarter, there are financial data attached to that forecast. Also, understanding your financial picture is important when preparing your tax returns. Every business idea leads to a business decision, and those decisions create your financial forms and outlook. In this section, you will learn about your financial statements.

READ YOUR FINANCIAL STATEMENTS

As a small business owner, it is important to have a clear understanding of your financial picture. Therefore, if you are scared of the data, begin by balancing the checkbook, and reading the financial statement. Your goal is to understand what the information is telling you about the state of your organization.

I recommend you track your sales on a daily or weekly basis. This will help you reconcile the bank statements. You also want to review your statements before your accountant receives them. From time to time I will receive a phone call from my financial team, inquiring about a transaction. I love that I can share that information with them. By understanding your financial statements, and being able to communicate with your accountant or other financial team members, you are showcasing how important the understanding of your financial picture is to you as the business owner. You are also setting an example for the rest of your team.

Financial policies

As a small business owner, it is also important to set clear financial policies and stick with them. These policies should include billing and collection of your receivables. If you are working with an accountant, have them set up your initial accounting system. Sit down with them and get a clear understanding of how it works. Most importantly, don't be afraid to ask questions. There are no secrets, as it relates to your business.

Accounting Systems

As we begin this section, we will focus on providing an understanding of the Accounting systems. Accounting systems revolve around three important elements: assets, liabilities, and owner's equity. Assets are what your business owns. Liabilities are what your business owes. Owner's equity is what you have invested in the business. For large organizations, this is often referred to as capital or net worth.

When you think of a method for recording your financial information, double-entry accounting records the entry once as a debit, to one account, and a credit to another account. When you think about your business, you want to think about your finances using the following accounting equations:

Assets = Liabilities + Owner's equity

For this equation, Assets= Liabilities + Owner's Equity is the basis of the balance sheet. Any entry made on the debit side of the balance sheet should also be credited on the credit side of the balance sheet, to maintain a balance.

Profit = Revenue – Expenses

Profit = Revenue – Expenses, represents the activity described on the income statement. The revenue you keep equals the money you brought in, minus what you have to spend.

Cash flow = Receipts – Disbursements

Cash flow = receipts – disbursements is the basis of the cash flow statement. The funding you have on hand at any given time equals the money you bring in, minus what you have to payout. Now, I will provide information on two types of accounting methods that you can use to record transactions.

Cash Basis or Accrual Accounting.

One of the most important decisions you will make for your business is, deciding whether to use an accrual or cash basis accounting system. The difference between the two relates to how you will document the timing of your receipts and disbursements.

When using the cash basis accounting system, you or your accountant will record income and expenses when the money is received.   If you receive an order for $10,000 in February, but do not receive payment until April, the $10,000 is a credit on your April statement.

When looking at the accrual basis of accounting, income, and expenses, are counted at the time of the transaction.   A $10,000 order received in February, would be listed as income earned in February.   If the income is never received, additional accounting entries would be made to write off the loss.

When determining your method, it is important to have a conversation with your tax professional and your accountant. You want to think about the growth of your business and business formation when making your decision. Understanding the importance of your financial picture is also important when creating your business plan.   You will notice after reading this book, that many business functions overlap, and are relevant in many areas of your business.

Accounting Records

Next, I want to speak about records you should keep.   One of the terms you want to understand is the generally accepted accounting principles (GAAP).   The guidelines are designed to ensure that regardless of the business type, the organization follows financial standards that are uniformly accepted across many industries.

It is also important to know that your accounting begins when you record your raw data from sources, such as purchase orders, check stubs, and sales slips into a journal, excel spreadsheet, or accounting software, such as Quickbooks, Quickbooks Pro, or Mint.

You may want to use several journals for cash receipts, purchases, and cash disbursements.

You may also use a general ledger, which is a summary book for recording all transactions and account balances. You can also find software that allows you to create these documents as well. Attached is a photo of a ledger created in excel. This gives you an idea of the types of expenses you want to track for your business.

GENERAL LEDGER

Account Title	Actual	Budgeted	Remaining
Revenue	$100,000	$150,000	$ 50,000
Advertising Expense	$ 5,000	$ 10,000	$ 5,000
Printer	$ 5,000	$ 10,000	$ 5,000
Medical	$ 20,000	$ 30,000	$ 10,000
Office Expense	$ 5,000	$ 10,000	$ 5,000
Insurance	$ 5,000	$ 3,000	($ 2,000)
Marketing	$ 10,000	$ 5,000	($ 5,000)
Charitables	$ 5,000	$ 10,000	$ 5,000
Office Equipment	$ 5,000	$ 10,000	$ 5,000

Business Forms

As you begin to think about your business, you want to

become familiar with several types of financial forms. For a new business owner, I have listed some of the most important forms with definitions.

Income Statement

An income statement is one of the three major financial statements that report your company's financial performance over a specific period. See the below income statement created in excel.

INCOME STATEMENT

Name

Time Period

Revenue
    Gross Sales
    Less: Sales Returns and Allowances
    Net Sales

Cost of Goods Sold
    Beginning Inventory
    Add Purchases
    Direct Labor
    Freight-in
    Indirect Expenses
    Inventory Available
    Less: Ending Inventory

Cost of Goods Sold

Gross Profit (Loss)

Expenses
Advertising
Amortization
Bad Debts
Bank Charges
Charitable Contributions
 Depreciation
Dues and Subscriptions
Insurance
Interest
Legal and Professional
Office Expense
Payroll Taxes
Postage
Rent
Repairs and Maintenance
Supplies
Telephone
Travel
Utilities
Wages

Total Expenses

Net Operating Income

Gain (Loss) on Sales of Assets

Interest Income

Total Other Income

Net Income (Loss)

When looking at your income statement, you want to focus on your net income. Net Income = (Total Revenue + gains) –(Total Expenses+losses). Your total revenue is the sum of both operating and non-operating revenues, while total expenses include those incurred by all of your business activities.

Operating revenue is the revenue earned based on your primary activities. For example, a t-shirt company's revenue is earned based on the number of t-shirts sold. Non-Operating Revenue, are revenue realized through secondary business activities. Revenue in this category may consist of interest earned from business capital or rental income from a business property. For any potential investors or bank loan officers, an income statement provides valuable insights into a company's operations, the efficiency of management, and performance relative to industry peers.

The balance sheet

The balance sheet provides an instant snapshot of your business at any given moment. A balance sheet has two major sections. One showing the assets, and the other showing the liabilities and owner's equity of the business. Please see a sample balance sheet you can recreate in excel.

YOUR COMPANY NAME

BALANCE SHEET

Assets

Current assets: Previous Year

Current Year

Cash

Investments

Inventories

Accounts receivable

Pre-paid expenses

Other

Total current assets

Fixed Assets

Property and equipment

Leasehold improvements

Equity and other investments

Less accumulated depreciation

Total fixed assets

Total assets

Liabilities and owner's equity

Current liabilities: Previous Year

Current Year

Accounts payable

Accrued wages

Accrued compensation

Income taxes payable

Unearned revenue

Other

Total current liabilities

Long Term Liabilities

Mortgage payable

Total long-term liabilities

Owner's Equiity

Investment capital

Accumulated retained earnings

Total owner's equity

Total liabilities and owner's equity

Balance

The next financial statement important for a small business owner is the Cash-Flow Statement. The cash flow statement summarizes the cash coming into, and going out of, your business. The importance of tracking and forecasting your cash flow is difficult to overstate because it is critical to the survival of the business. New businesses will often show a profit, but have problems paying their bills. Please see the following abbreviated cash flow statement divided into sections. This form can be reproduced in Microsoft Excel.

ABBREVIATED CASH FLOW STATEMENT

	JAN	FEB	MAR	APR	MAY	JUN	JUL	AUG
Cash on hand								
Cash receipts								
Cash Sales								
Returns and allowances								
Collections on A/R								
Interst Income								
Owner Contributions								
SUBTOTAL								
TOTAL CASH								

In this section, you want to review your financial picture which will help you understand how much cash is coming into your business monthly. By understanding your cash position, this helps you identify all available cash resources. I used this area to project my monthly revenue. This would identify whether the revenue was coming from a training workshop or from book sales.

CASH PAID OUT	JAN	FEB	MAR	APR	MAY	JUN	JUL	AUG
Advertusubg								
Commission and fees								
Contract labor								
Employee benefit programs								
Interest Expense								
Materials and supplies (COG)								
Utilities								
Mortage								
Office Expense								
Rent								
Travel								
Wages								
SUBTOTAL								

In this section, it is important to list cash that is paid out of the business. Listed above are some of the standard monthly expenses incurred by small business owners. I used this section to monitor my monthly expenses. It was here, I discovered I could create savings by converting some monthly expenses to yearly expenses.

Long-term Expenses	JAN	FEB	MAR	APR	MAY	JUN	JUL	AUG
Capital expenses								
Loan Principal Payments								
Other Expenses								
SUBTOTAL								
TOTAL CASH PAID OUT								

In this section you want to list long term payments. I used this section to monitor capital equipment for my embroidery and heat press machines.

OTHER DATA	JAN	FEB	MAR	APR	MAY	JUN	JUL	AUG
Sales volume								
Accts Receivable Balance								
Bad debt								
Inventory on hand								
Accounts Payable balance								
Depreciation								

In the final section, you can track other relevant financial data for your business, such as inventory, accounts recievable balances, or bad debt incurred by your business. I used this section to track inventory, or bad debt. By tracking it monthly, it helps when reconciliing year end reports, but allows you to understand the financial picture for your operation.

Using Your Financial statement

As you begin to think about your financial statements, I want to provide you with a checklist for managing your business.

Daily

1. Check your bank balance.

2. Calculate daily summaries of sales and cash receipts.

3. Note any problems in your credit collections.

4. Record money paid out.

Weekly

1. When managing your cash flow, use a spreadsheet for recording receipts and disbursements. The importance of this step is to see what is going on with your business, and it helps you identify cash deficiencies.

2. Note slow paying accounts receivable.

3. Note discounts offered for your accounts payable.

4. Calculate the accumulation of hours worked, and total payroll owed.

5. Note when taxes are due, and which reports are required.

Monthly

1. If you are using an outside accounting firm, provide records of your receipts, bank accounts, and journals.

2. Review your income statement.

3. Review your balance sheet.

4. Reconcile your business checking account.

5. Balance your petty cash account.

6. Review federal tax requirements.

7. Review your accounts receivable.

Understanding your financials will be a great benefit for you moving forward.

11

Preparing for Globalization

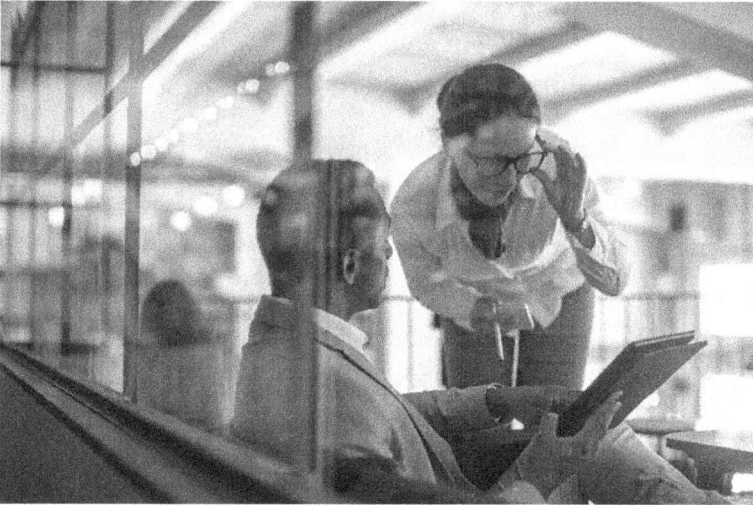

In this chapter, I want to focus on growth. Growth in this context is turning your small business into a large enterprise. Now as you think about growth, you want to think about expanding into other markets. Going global requires that we look at how we can expand. This process might require you to think about selling your product internationally.

The key point that I want to make here is, that business growth is about business expansion and creating an effective growth strategy. To begin, it is important to transform your thinking. Going global and expanding business growth is about transforming your mindset.

When you transform your mindset, you begin to view your business differently. You will take on the attitude of large business leaders. You will stop looking at your business as just a small business, but a growing enterprise. For example, your first step towards growth might be finding office space and paying rent. For many business owners, this is a huge step. Therefore, I want to provide a step-by-step process for growth that focuses on intensive and integrative growth strategies.

Intensive Growth

As I begin to look at the impact of an intensive growth strategy, I begin to focus on the 4 Ps of marketing taught in college. The 4 P's of marketing focus on the product, price, placement, and promotion. These basic principles, along with some other strategies, can be used to create your growth strategy.

Market Penetration

Market penetration is a strategy you can expand by focusing on how to sell more of your products to your current customers. This strategy recommends you find more ways for your customers to use your products. Green Mountain Coffee Roasters, introduced the K-cups for Coffee, and now we can purchase K-cups for tea, hot chocolate, and soup.

When I think about my own company, I started with leadership training and personal development. In order for me to achieve better market penetration, I added book publishing services and team building products to my corporate offerings. I used a market penetration strategy of thinking of more ways to provide my services to clients.

Market Development

The next area that I want to focus on is Market Development. Market development is a growth strategy that identifies and develops new market segments for current and new products. For my company, I hired trainers and speakers in other towns to conduct my training and leadership development workshops. Also, by using a leasing company with global office locations, I can reserve an office or conference room to meet with clients as I travel.

Expand Distribution Channels

A distribution channel is a process where you expand your delivery methods for getting your product into the hands of current and new customers. I can admit this one can be challenging. For my company, the pandemic eliminated in-person training sessions. I had to use different methods like Zoom and Microsoft Teams to expand my distribution channel.

If you only sell your product locally, creating a website or placing your products on Amazon, Etsy, and Shopify, can expand your reach to a different group of customers. If you sell a service, think about online platforms where you can advertise, thus expanding your distribution channel.

New Product Offerings

Sometimes a market condition requires the business owner to introduce a new product to customers. One of the best examples is the creation of tablets by computer companies. The tablet was a standalone device that could function as a computer. For Apple and Samsung this was a huge win. Amazon would respond with the expansion of its E-Reader, the Kindle Fire. Each tablet was sold for a different price and catered to a particular market. The products are still evolving and additional vendors have now entered the marketplace, helping to maintain competition.

As you move forward with your intensive growth strategies, remember to take it one step at-a-time. You want to look at each area, and move forward at a pace you can control as the business owner. Also, after a good internal review of your organization, you may find the strategy supports growth or is needed for survival.

Integrative Growth Strategies

The next area I want to cover is the Integrative Growth Strategies. Integrative Growth Strategies focus on acquisition or integration of the business.

Horizontal

A Horizontal growth strategy involves buying a competing business. This strategy can add to your company's growth but also eliminates competition. Often when companies buy competing businesses, they focus on the innovation created by the other brand, and also recognize the potential increase in their market share.

Backward Strategy

This strategy focuses on buying a supplier as a way of controlling the supply chain. This strategy could support the development of a product faster or cheaper. It is often a strategy used by manufacturing firms, but could also work for your particular industry.

Acquisitions

Another integrative strategy is acquisitions. Acquisitions can also be focused on buying component companies that are associated with your distribution chain. For example, a t-shirt manufacturer may want to purchase a local retail store to push their products and gain a competitive edge. Intimate Brands Inc. is an excellent example. Intimate Brands owns Bath & Body Works, Victoria Secrets, and Gryphon Development.

Diversification

Another integrative strategy focuses on diversification. Often when people think of diversification, they think of their 401K portfolio. However, diversification can be used as an effective business strategy. Here, the business owner grows their company by buying another company, unrelated to their business. Amazon is a great example. Amazon purchased Whole Foods, Twitch, and Kiva Systems, which is a robotics company, to diversify their holdings.

As you are reviewing growth strategies for your business, remember that growth strategies will not be created overnight. Business owners must be willing to change course in response to feedback from the marketplace. As a business owner, success demands that you explore all options at all times.

Managing your Cash Flow

As a small business owner, it is important to understand how much cash you have coming in monthly and what's the cycle for your bills. When taking a Dave Ramsey course several years ago, he mentioned that for your household, we needed to create an emergency fund. It is also important to create this type of fund for your business. You want to have 3 to 6 months of funds to cover expenses. This became important, as many businesses were facing the effects of the 2020 pandemic.

As a business owner, it is also important to be able to negotiate monthly costs. Every year, I contact the phone company about my corporate plan and I challenge them to provide me with better rates or risk losing my business to a competitor. I also changed my payment plans for my website, graphic programs, and email accounts, from monthly to monthly. This change provided a significant savings for the company. This is important when looking at subscription services, e-commerce, or other monthly plans you may have. Organizations provide a discount if you convert from a monthly to a yearly plan.

Follow Your Intuition

All business owners must master the talent of using their gut. Your gut, is your internal intuition or feeling. If you feel uneasy about a business decision, slow down and take time to re-examine it. This could be your intuition at work. This gut instinct may also kick in win identifying a great opportunity that no one else recognizes. Here are some examples where individuals followed their intuition and reaped great rewards.

Google

Google was co-founded by Larry Page and Sergey Brin while they were attending Stanford University. They almost gave up on the idea, because it was taking up a lot of their time. They trusted their business intuition and took a big risk by purchasing YouTube. Now Youtube has become one of their best acquisitions.

Square

Square was co-founded by Jack Dorsey. Square started with a card reader that allowed businesses to conduct financial transactions. Jack trusted his intuition and branched out into payroll services. Now, one of his best products is the widely known and widely used, Cash App. This app allows individuals to electronically exchange money using their mobile devices. The cash app has become another valuable tool for small business owners.

Amazon

One of the companies that I love to talk about in University settings is Amazon. Jeff Bazos, started Amazon in 1994 as an online e-commerce site to sell books. Jeff would trust his intuition and expand Amazon's product offerings into selling electronics, apparel, cloud-based computing services and currently over 12 million other products. The company has now expanded into Movies and Music. In 2017, Jeff purchased Whole Foods, which has a unique business model. Jeff's intuition has translated into great rewards.

Henry Ford

While facing falling demand for his vehicles and massive employee turnover, Henry Ford trusted his business intuition and doubled the salary of his employees. This action, thought by other industry titans, would surely drown a company already in free fall.

Within a year, productivity doubled and employee turnover dropped significantly. These same employees were now able to afford and purchase the very vehicles that they were making. Ford's intuition had proved the logic of the industry titans wrong. All of these examples were of individuals that used their gut intuition to capitalize on great business ideas, or avert impending disaster.

Delegation

Another key area of focus when creating your integrative strategy is understanding the impact of delegation. Delegation is simply shifting the authority of a task or a function from one individual to another. Delegation allows the business owner to assign to others, less important tasks, which frees them up to focus on big picture ideas. Delegation can also be used as part of your employee motivation strategy, which allows you to empower your staff.

Delegating may also expose the need to hire new employees. This can be challenging when small business owners are trying to control their cost, yet understanding that their need for expansion is critical for growth.

When its all said and done, learning how to delegate effectively will be a major tool in your toolbelt. The following are a few tips to help you while delegating. First, provide complete and clear instructions while delegating. If employees have to come back to you several times with questions, you will have defeated your purpose for the delegation.

Second, do not expect perfection from your employees. Some of the delegated tasks may be new to the employee. As the business owner, establish standards and time frames, yet be flexible in your expectations. Create an atmosphere of empowerment, feedback, and trust. This will allow your employees to grow and increase in knowledge and ability.

Lastly, resist the idea that you are the only person capable of doing the work. As business owners, we are passionate about what we have created and sometimes the fear of trusting others keeps us from delegating duties. This robs us of that needed time to dream big, explore possibilities, and research new ideas.

Obtain Legal Advice

I intentionally saved this topic for last, because I truly believe it is the most important item in this section. Obtaining legal advice is a form of insurance that every business owner should purchase. Legal experts protect us from lawsuits, damages, and other unknown pitfalls. They are knowledgeable about the laws of the land, and they help you manage risk. Everything that you have worked for, and invested in, can all be lost by failing to get good legal counsel. When creating contracts, signing leases for rent, or looking at the format for your business, it is important to obtain the advice of a legal professional. In order to keep your cost low, you may want to place your lawyer on retainer or pay as you go. Remember, protecting your investment is of the highest importance.

CREATING A GLOBAL STRATEGY

In this section, I would like to revisit the possibility of selling your product, or service, internationally. Expanding globally can be a scary endeavor. However, with a global strategy, you can reap incredible rewards for your business. According to the Small Business Administration, 96 percent of consumers live outside of the United States. That is an important statistic as you think about your product or service.

The SBA affirms that many of these opportunities are within

a Small Business Owner's Reach. One of the best resources available is the Small Business Administration's (SBA) website. The site is full of information. One of the Programs provided by the SBA is the State Trade Expansion Program. This program provides grants to states and territories to add small business export services. This program is managed locally so it will be important to reach out to your local SBA office. Also located on the SBA's website, is a link showing you the awardees for each state. Here you can contact the awardee for additional information.

If you are willing to take on the challenge of going global, it will be imperative that you take a crash course in demographics and marketing. If 96 percent of the business is taking place outside the United States, then it is important to you, as a business owner, to recognize and understand population growth. This information can help you with determining where you want to expand your product offerings.

One website I love to visit is the CIA World Factbook. This site provides information on Countries. You can learn about a country's demographics, trade products, and economic standing. This is important information when looking to expand your business internationally. One last website that I recommend that you visit is the International Trade Administration. This website provides additional information on expanding your reach internationally.

The final area that I want to focus on is Global Marketing. Global Marketing allows businesses to promote their product or service to customers internationally. It includes an understanding of market research, advertising, and customer segmentation. The first step I recommend is choosing your overseas market location. With international expansion, selection of the country or region is important. You must conduct some research on culture, economics, and politics. You also want to know about your own host country's relationship with the industry. This will be useful in helping you understand risk.

The next step recommends that you conduct market research. Market research provides clear data on demographics, customer needs, and competition. You want to speak to customers and view websites to evaluate the competitiveness of your products. The Department of Commerce's website will provide you with resources in this area.

In my marketing classes, I teach students about primary and secondary research. Primary research focuses on initial sources of information such as customers, government representatives, and communicating with decision-makers in the desired location. Your secondary market research will include articles, statistical data, and trade data. All of this information can assist you when making your decision.

Another advantage we learn in Global Marketing, is to establish a corporate representative in the area. You may need to take a trip overseas or hire someone who is working and living in the region. This person can provide first-hand knowledge of what is happening in the region and leverage their contacts to help you. They can also provide information on the economy, products, politics, and competition.

Now, I would like to discuss the subject of competition. Considerable research is necessary for this area. When expanding globally it is important to understand the host country's competitors. With global expansion, the key is profitability and survival. You want to understand what will work for your business. This may include the prices for your products, packaging, and the product's name. For example, what works in the United States may not work in India. You will need to have a good understanding of India's customs, economy, and political environment. This will prevent you from accidentally offending customers or dignitaries in that region.

The next step in taking your product global is asking for assistance. Here the business owner needs to reach out to others operating in that marketplace. I recommend you make a list of your region's competitors. Your goal here is to study their products and services while looking for possible industry-related partnerships.

The final step in global marketing is to create an export strategy. In your export plan, you want to identify your business goals, financing strategy, and how you will sell your products overseas. You must also determine how you will hire your personnel. To be successful, you may need to use local recruiters to place ads on local internet job boards. You may find you need to hire a translator to help with language issues. Or you may want to add different language options for your products on your website.

If you are selling a product online, are there tax laws, or other business-related issues you should plan for? Last, but not least, if you are selling a product, what do you need to know about the supply chain or distribution outlets? This information is critical and cannot be overlooked. In my economics class, students engage in a business simulation. In this simulation, they have to create the product, hire a sales staff, choose their market, create a marketing strategy, and compete against their classmates.

It is an excellent exercise because they have to think like a business owners. Going global is about business expansion. Therefore, conduct solid market research, and join trade associations. Research and work with governmental agencies that specialize in these areas. When you put clear metrics in place, you can effectively expand your products or services globally.

12

Government Contracts

In this section, we will focus on selling your product or service to government agencies. The government in the United States purchases trillions of dollars in products and services. A significant portion is at the federal level.

Government contracts can add significant growth to your business, especially here in the United States. For developing nations, understanding what their government purchases, and how they purchase those resources, can also be beneficial.

To be successful in obtaining a government contract, it is important to understand local, state, and federal purchasing guidelines. Each group has its policies and rules. The government has also divided contractors into two categories, prime contractors or subprime contractors. Prime contractors bid and win contracts directly from the federal government. Subcontractors partner with prime contractors and may provide a particular resource relative to a contract.

Also, depending on the business structure, this can open the door to securing a contract, as the government reserves about 23% of contracts for certain business types. The business types that fall into this category are woman-owned, disadvantaged, veteran-owned, native Americans, or those that are located in particular hub zones.

These businesses can also receive assistance to help them with securing a government contract. By understanding the process of selling to the government, you can apply the same strategy for other institutions. The key contracts that I want to focus on in this section are contracts set aside for particular groups.

SET ASIDE CONTRACTS

Set aside contracts are designed to assist small businesses in doing business with the federal government. These contracts are designed to assist small businesses in competing in the global marketplace. The government provides two types of set-aside contracts and they are competitive and sole source. Competitive set-aside contracts are several businesses who each provide a product or perform a service. These contracts are usually under $150,000. These contracts are usually for women-owned, veteran-owned, minority-owned, HUBZone, or 8 (a) businesses.

Sole source set aside contracts are for businesses who government agencies believe are the sole provider of a particular service. These types of contracts are used by many local government departments. They can also be issued without going through a competitive bidding process.

To begin doing business with the government, please check the requirements with your local, state, and federal agencies. You will be required to register your business in order to become a vendor. One of the most important points in selling to the city, state, or federal government, is having all your business paperwork in order.

Depending on the state, there may be a cost to access bids, but this process can also open your business to more contracting exposure. If you want to do business with the federal government, please register your business with the (SAM) System for Award Management, and you will be able to participate in all contracting programs your business is qualified for.

Another important process when working with the government is obtaining key certifications that support your business type. These certifications can open the door to prime contracts. They are useful in helping the government identify firms who not only say they meet a certain requirement, but have the documentation to validate their claim. Please visit certify.sba.gov to learn about certification programs for your business.

13

Leadership

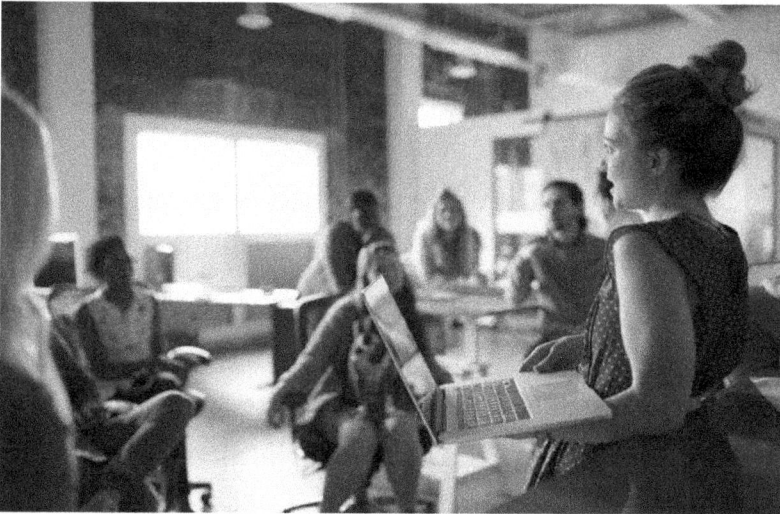

As we conclude this book, I want to focus on an important topic for running a business and that is leadership. Leadership is a fascinating topic that impacts all human experiences.

Excellence in leadership requires the ability to attract people, motivate them to give their best efforts, and solve problems.

All new business owners often start their enterprise as a solopreneur and then later realize that it is time to expand. The stages that new business owners travel through are emergence, existence, success, takeoff, and maturity. Each phase represents a change in the business and requires clear leadership and management. As an entrepreneurial leader, you will focus on guiding your team through innovation, operation, and inspiration.

As a certified leadership expert, I have learned through research and training that leadership is about influence. Leadership is the process by which a person exerts influence over others. The leader can inspire, motivate, and direct their activities to achieve goals. As an entrepreneur, leadership will be important to the growth of your business.

Often, in an academic setting, I love to debate whether leaders are born or made. Some people say leaders are born and some say leaders are made. I believe that people can have inborn characteristics that support their rise as leaders. However, based on experience, I have seen people who are persistent, passionate, driven, and disciplined, rise to leadership. Their success is connected to their understanding of their internal characteristics and their style of leadership. Let's begin with a discussion of leadership styles and traits.

Leadership is often defined by, leadership styles and traits. Some leaders are identified as transformational figures. These leaders help their employees see that their jobs and performance are important to the organization. They also help their subordinates see the need to improve their personal and professional development. Most importantly, transformational leaders help their employees work to support the company's goals and objectives.

Another form of leaders are identified as being transactional leaders. These leaders use their power or position to encourage high performance. These types of leaders also use their power as a way to reprimand low performers. Thus, transactional in the exchange between the manager and the employee. I am sure, if we all think back over our careers, we can identify individuals who have inspired us to give more of ourselves. We also can remember the individuals who were so bad at leadership, that they forced us to find another job or start our own business based on the experience.

As a leader, it is important to define your leadership qualities. It begins by asking a simple question. What does it take to be a successful leader, and what is the most effective leadership style? Research within academia has produced many models of leadership, but ultimately many experts believe leadership is connected to trait leadership and behavior.

The trait model of leadership focuses on personal characteristics that cause effective leadership. Some traits identified as effective for leaders include decisiveness, communication, self-awareness, and generosity. Research suggests that having these traits provide a great path to exceptional leadership. In the pages to follow, we will examine each trait, and provide some advice on how to identify your traits as a leader.

Decisiveness

As a new business owner, one of your first challenges will include making clear decisions. It will be important to remember that as a business owner, your decisions may be firm, difficult, authoritative, and timely. Therefore when making business decisions, apply flexibility and logic to your decisions. Resist the need to make impulsive decisions related to your business.

I also find that when making decisions, we have to let past mistakes go. We have to focus on what we have learned from the decision and use that to scale the business as we move forward. Finally, you must make a decision and commit to that decision.

I can remember when I purchased my first embroidery machine. I purchased a machine that was for sewing and embroidery. I did not think about the growth of the business when making this decision. If I would have spent a little bit more time researching, or discussed this decision with an advisor, I would have discovered that buying an industrial machine for an additional $2,000 would have been a better business decision. This impulsive decision forced me to have to buy two machines and spend additional business resources.

One great business decision I made was to learn screen printing and embroidery. This allowed me to use my equipment for small orders and subcontract my large orders. I also learned the business and improved my negotiation skills, now understanding the costs of thread, screen printing ink, t-shirts, and labor.

Communication

The next area I want to focus on is communication. Communication is very important for a leader. It is a key skill for how leaders accomplish goals every day. Excellent communicators inspire people. Great communicators understand the importance of connecting with people. They understand the importance of creating a relationship with their followers. Great communicators understand the importance of storytelling and understand the impact of visuals when crafting their message. When you craft a good message, your followers can internalize the vision and make it their own.

Great Communicators also understand the importance of speaking to groups. They understand the importance of intimacy in their approach. They are gifted in crafting a message where the listener believes they are only communicating with them.

Generosity

If you want to lead exceptionally, it is important to understand the impact of generosity. When a leader is generous, they engage in sharing credit and understand the impact of offering enthusiastic praise for their employees. As a leader, you must be as committed to your employees success, as you are to your own. Great leaders will encourage all of their followers to achieve their personal best. This not only benefits the company, but the employee and the team.

Self-Awareness

Self Awareness is a key component of emotional intelligence. Emotional intelligence is a skill that many top performers possess. Great leaders who have high self-awareness, have a clear accurate image of their leadership style, strengths, and weaknesses. They also know how to use their knowledge in this area and motivate followers who may not be as adept.

LEADERSHIP PRODUCTIVITY

Now that we have shared information on leadership styles and traits, I wanted to provide some tips that will improve your leadership productivity. Here are some tips to add to your toolbelt.

Maximize your minutes – There are 1440 minutes in each day. We have seen people lose money and recapture it on the same day. However, lost time can never be reclaimed. As you plan your day, look at your time in minutes and not hours, to ensure you are maximizing your time.

Focus – Robert Kiyosaki, has a very famous quote, " Follow one course until successful". This is important when looking at your daily tasks. Sometimes multi-tasking may not be effective. Therefore, identify your most important tasks daily, and rank them in the level of importance.

Maximize Your Calendar – For busy working professionals it is important to keep track of priorities. Many of us have used the, to-do list, but that may not work for a small business owner. I recommend that you place all your tasks on your calendar. You can reschedule items that have not been completed. If you are using an electronic calendar, you can change the due date, and have all your important information located in one place

Use your tablet or carry a notebook – One very helpful technique is taking notes. When I take notes, I can free my mind, but I also can review the information. There have been times when my notebooks saved me in business. Therefore carry a notebook or use your IPAD to write down key things you need to remember.

Use the 80/20 Rule The 80/20 rule taken from the Pareto Principle states that 80 percent of results come from 20 percent of the activities. Understanding this concept will help you understand which business activities will drive your greatest results.

Schedule Time for Email – Busy small business owners, cannot review emails throughout the day and remain on task. Therefore identify a time, when you can review emails and return phone calls. This can also be a task that you can be delegated to a subordinate, freeing you up for big-ticket items.

Create a morning routine. It is important when you begin your day that you engage in a consistent routine. This can include exercise, a healthy breakfast, inspirational reading, or journaling. You want to get in the habit of feeding yourself mentally, and spiritually, so you can feed others.

I have shared several tips on understanding the importance of leadership. Please take a moment to answer the following questions. This questionnaire will help you identify your leadership skills and traits.

What do you think are the most important traits of a leader?

_____

_____

_____

_____

_____

List some examples of leaders you admire? What can you learn from them, that will improve your leadership skills?

_____

_____

_____

_____

Do you think you possess the qualities people want in a leader? If yes, which ones? If no, where can you improve?

_____

_____

_____

_____

_____

As I complete this final chapter, my mind goes back to the early days, when starting my business. I had no blueprint to follow, which forced me to learn along the way. I was thrown into situations, where I had to save myself from drowning. However, I also learned that I had many gifts to share with this world. One of my gifts is sharing this book with you.

As you move forward into starting your business, be open to success. Trust your instincts and surround yourself with positive mentors who can support you. I hope you use this step-by-step blueprint to create the business of your dreams. If nothing else, know that I believe in you, and you should too. After all, your success is my business.

About the Author

Dr. Regina Banks-Hall, DBA SHRM – CP is the Founder of RBH Professional Development Institute, LLC. RBH Professional Development Institute empowers individuals and corporations with specialized training, customized to help individuals discover their unique gifts and talents. The company also provides book publishing and small business coaching services. Dr. Regina Banks-Hall, is an internationally published author, professor, trainer, business coach, motivational speaker and business strategist. She is currently the Dean of Graduate & Professional Studies for Cleary University. Among her many accomplishments, Dr. Regina has been recognized by Toastmasters International as an Distinguished Toastmaster. Dr. Banks-Hall serves on the PWN International Advisory Board. She has been certified by the Society of Human Resource Management as a SHRM Certified Professional, certified by the Professional Woman Network as a Holistic Life Coach, and is a certified speaker, teacher, trainer and coach with the John Maxwell Team. Dr. Banks-Hall has a Bachelor's of Arts Degree in Business Management, Master's Degree in Human Resource Management, and a Doctorate Degree in Leadership. Dr. Banks-Hall serves on several public and private, advisory and school boards. Her mission in life is simply to serve others. To book Dr. Regina Banks-Hall for keynote presentations, seminars, professional development workshops, or vision board workshops, please contact her (866) 600-6322. You can send correspondence addressed to RBH Professional Development Institute, 2000 Town Center, 19th Floor, Southfield, MI 48075. You can also email her at regina@rbankshall.com

Appendix

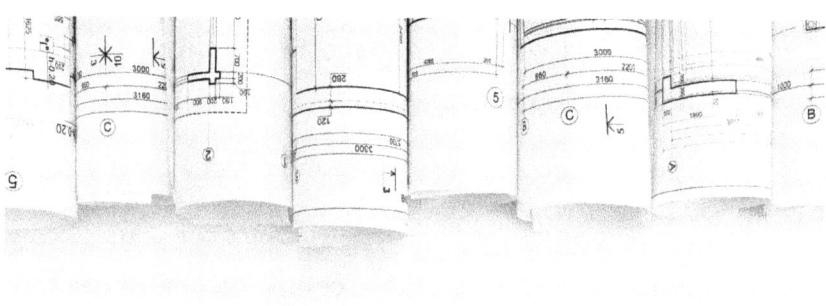

YOUR STEP-BY-STEP BLUEPRINT

- Select your business name. Perform a corporate name search to make sure your name is still available.

- Register a domain name and secure social media profiles for the company.

- Apply for an EIN with the IRS and local or state business licenses.

- Open a business bank account and apply for a business credit card.

- Find the appropriate space to use as your primary business location.

- Once a location is secured, get services set up in the business name, including primary phone number and other necessary utilities.

- Decide on a legal structure: Corporation, LLC or Sole Proprietorship.

- Get your website up and running.

- Set up an accounting and record-keeping system or hire an accountant.

- Select an accounting system and select a fiscal year.

- Evaluate and select needed insurance for your business: liability, workers' compensation, or health insurance.

- Prepare and begin networking with marketing materials (business cards, brochures, media ads).

- Create a good public relations campaign.

- Introduce your new business to your local community and your social media networks.

Resources

Resources	Website link
Amazon	www.amazon.com
Angie's List	www.angieslist.com
Apple	www.apple.com
Ben & Jerry's Ice Cream	www.benjerrys.com
Better business bureau	www.bbbonline.org
Cash App	https://cashapp
Census Bureau	www.census.gov
Chewy	www.chewy.com
CIA World Factbook	www.cia.gov
Competitive Strategy by Michael Porter	http://www.isc.hbs.edu
Costco	www.costco.com
Dave Ramsey	www.daveramsey.com
Ebay	www.ebay.com
Etsy	www.etsy.com
Facebook	www.facebook.com
Ford Motor Company	www.ford.com
Google	www.google.com
Green Mountain Coffee Roasters	www.keurig.com
Henry Ford	www.history.com/topics/inventions/henry-ford
Indiegogo	www.indiegogo.com
International Trade Administration	www.trade.gov
Intimate Brands	
Kabbage	www.kabbage.com
Kickstarter	www.kickstarter.com
Microsoft Teams	www.teams.microsoft.com

Mint	www.mint.com
National association for women business owners	www.nawbo.org
National Federation of Independent Business (NFIB)	www.nfib.com
Pareto Principle	
Quickbooks Pro	www.intuit.com
PayPal	www.paypal.com
Pinterest	www.pinterest.com
Ring	www.ring.com
Robert Kiyosaki	www.richdad.com
Ruth Chris	www.ruthschris.com
SAM System for Award (SAM)	https://sam.gov/SAM/pages/public/index.jsf
Sam's Club	www.samsclub.com
Samsung	https://www.samsung.com/us
SCORE	www.score.org
Shopify	www.shopify.com
Small Business Administration	www.sba.gov
Small Business Management – Tim Hatton	
South Dakota vs. Wayfair	https://supreme.justia.com/cases/federal/us/585/17-494/
Square	www.square.com
Square	https://squareup.com
Survey Monkey	www.surveymonkey.com
The American Heart Association	www.heart.org
The World bank	www.worldbank.org
Tik Tok	www.tiktok.com
Toastmasters	www.toastmasters.org

Tumblr	www.tumbler.com
Twitch	www.twitch.tv
Twitter	www.twitter.com
Warby Parker	www.warbyparker.com
Whole Foods	www.wholefoodsmarket.com
WordPress	www.wordpress.com
Yelp	www.yelp.com
Zoom	www.zoom.com